This book is dedicated to all of the victims and survivors of abuse.

Acknowledgments

Saving Lives Through Lit would like to thank everyone who saw fit, took a chance and believed in our vision to join in with us. To those of you that had a part in our first anthology being published; from the many authors, writers and poets who contributed their talented piece, to the businesses that provided their services. Voices Behind the Tears would not have come off as well as it did without your help and assistance.

This project is more than a one-time affair. We have big dreams, plans and goals and it moves us immensely that you share in this vision. Domestic violence & abuse in all its ugly forms, from child abuse, to sexual abuse, emotional abuse and everything in between is a cancer that has been swept under too many rugs for centuries. With all the evolution that mankind has made, unfortunately we still blame the victims and shamefully protect the abusers.

S.L.T.L. thanks you all for standing up for the victims alongside of us. Whether man, woman or child, they now have yet another outlet to be heard. They have someone else who is dedicated to speaking up for their silent tears and dreadful fears.

Thank you isn't nearly enough to express the way we feel towards your support, yet it is a good beginning.

THANK YOU!

Table of Contents

Introduction 1

Robert Sells 3

Karen "Kaye" Stackfield 9

Tamari Campbell 15

G.P.A. 21

Michele Tooles 25

Elizabeth Funderbirk 31

Luna Charles 41

Carlet Horne 49

W. Kay Shabazz 57

Lavinia Thompson 65

Kelli "SongBird" Garden 73

Chamani J Carter 79

Tamyara Brown 87

Terrell Mercer 93

Tony "The Logical" Wade 101

Envy Red 109

Kiexiza Rodriquez 119

Joyce Oscar 129

C. Highsmith-Hooks 137

Charron Monaye 141

Taquila Thompson 149

Latisha N. Patterson	153
Mashawn Mickles	163
Meka Phoenix Carter	169
N.S. Ugezene	177
Poetic Swag	181
Magogani P.	189
Antoinette Lakey	199
Danielle "Dani" Taylor	209
Earnestine Moore	213
Laura Johnson	221
Final Thoughts	235

Introduction

Saving Lives Through Lit would like to thank you in advance for your support of our first anthology, Voices Behind the Tears. We hope that you will join us and help to open the ears, hearts and minds of those across the world to the abuse that occurs every day in our neighborhoods behind closed doors.

We, the founders of S.L.T.L., Elizabeth Funderbirk-Rowe and Kiexiza Rodriquez, had a vision which involved bringing together those in the literary community and the general public to raise awareness and to be the voice for those who suffer in silence alone. It is our goal to take the talents and skills of our literary peers and use them to affect change. We want to show those that may feel they have no way out of their situation that there is hope. So, we sent out an S.O.S. and to our amazement received an overwhelming response from fellow, writers, authors, designers, and editors who were more than willing to aid in our mission.

Saving Lives Through Lit plans to publish one to two books yearly, with the goal of bridging the gap between the victims and those that want to help. S.L.T.L. desires to open the minds of those that think the abused either don't want help, or must like the situations they are in. We will do this through both fictional and true life stories, donated by wonderful writers. These stories will expose the reader to the harsh realities of the hushed world that an abused person endures. We hope these stories will also show victory and give hope that there is an escape, various outlets for assistance, and the bold truth that everyone deserves better. Whether the stories deal with domestic violence, rape, child abuse, sexual abuse or the other many forms of abuse, you can be sure that they will move you emotionally.

We chose to release our first anthology in October, because it is national Domestic Violence Awareness month. Together with the other 28 contributors who wrote poems, stories, excerpts and inspirational pieces, we hope you will continue to support our efforts.

Please join us in our mission to "Save Lives Through Literature" by donating to help us not only put out great quality books, but to give back. A portion of the proceeds from all book sales will be donated to Our Heart Foundation, which is located on our website. Donations can also be given directly on our website and are allocated directly to Our Heart Foundation.

Please join with those from the literary community and help us Save Lives Through Literature One Book at a Time.

www.savinglivesthroughlit.org

Thank you very much for your time, Saving Lives Through Lit!

Liz & Kie

Robert Sells

Robert is an award-winning Christian poet, author, motivational speaker and spoken word artist. He has a strong psalmist anointing on his life. Robert has released his debut Christian Spoken Word CD, "The Heart of a Man", which is now available for purchase. Some of his work has been featured in the motion picture "Battered Clergy: From Victim to Victor". Robert's first book, "Words of Inspiration: A Collection of Poems for the One You Love", released in 2006, was selected as the WeAreFearless Online Book Club's Pick of the Month for July 2007. His second book, "Words of Inspiration: Speak Healing", was released in 2008. Robert and his wife, Marlas, are the co-founders of Words of Inspiration Ministries. Robert currently serves as the Creative Arts & Poetry Editor for Divine Inspirations Magazine and has ministered at several women, men, and youth conferences. He was featured on "The John Lanier Show", a syndicated Christian talk show, as well as the "I'm Just Sayin" Christian talk show on TCT Network, with host Pastor Dan Willis. Robert has been featured on the "Poetry Over Music" compilation CD series and "Blessed of the Midwest Mix Tape - Volume 1" CD compilation.

WHY I WROTE:

"I am committed to seeing this vicious silent crime of domestic violence completely destroyed. This current project is near and dear to my heart because my wife and a number of my friends are survivors of domestic violence. There are far too many women who keep silent for fear of them or their children losing their lives. So they have to live with the daily threat of death at the hands of their spouse or loved one."

LINKS:
www.robertsellsonline.com
www.facebook.com/anointedpoet
http://theanointedpoet.blogspot.com/
www.youtube.com/theanointedpoet
www.reverbnation.com/theanointedpoet

Because You Loved Me

Because you loved me,
I loved you too, at least I thought…
I did everything I could to take care of you;
I went to work,
brought a check home for you,
but all the while
I ignored the sign that said,
"Beware of you"
if I didn't do what I'm supposed to do.

I didn't see what the problem was.
I got up every day and went to work.
I never missed a day, I was never late
I brought in big money, I took care of you.
I even let you clean the house,
wash my clothes and cook for me;
While I yelled to you
"Watch the house while I go out
and hang with my friends."
I'd pick up women that didn't mind pleasing me
and I didn't care where it would end.
Isn't that what you wanted me to do?

And every once in a while,
when you weren't acting like I wanted you to,
I'd take a flare to you,
slap you once or twice - just to put a scare in you.
I knocked you down sometimes,
I even kicked and stepped on you.
Because of me you would go out of the house
with so much makeup on that
you looked like a mime.
But, that's only because
You asked me one more time
Why haven't I married you?

Saving Lives Through Lit

Well I did,
so what more do you want from me?
Everything that I did for you,
I did because you loved me.

But one day I got a hold of that book they call the Bible
and I began to see everything I wasn't doing.
I began to see myself as the "me" I always said I wouldn't be,
I saw I had gone down the wrong road too many times,
I saw that the "I Love you's"
I was saying I really didn't mean,
I saw that what I was doing to you was what I thought was right…
I thought it was right because I loved you.
As I read the Bible I saw that
I really didn't love you like you loved me.
I read how Jesus came to this earth
and died for you and I.
And then I saw where it says,
"As men we should love our wives
as Christ loved the church unconditionally."
Well, He loved the church enough to die
for people He didn't know,
He gave His life so that we can be free.
I now know what I didn't do;
A tear came to my eye as I realized
I never died for you,
even though you loved me.

I didn't love you,
I didn't even know how to love me.
I couldn't trust you
because I couldn't even trust me.
I couldn't be your best friend
because I wasn't even a friend to myself.
I couldn't even hold you in my arms
and offer you shelter from the rain,
protect you from the flaming arrows
that the devil shot at you again and again,

Voices Behind the Tears

because I didn't allow God to hold me.

You see, I learned that I wasn't ready to marry you.
I learned that even though I thought I loved you,
I wasn't trying to please you
even though you cared for me.
My spirit wasn't at ease with you…
Oh God, what have I done to you?
Jesus!!!

Lord I want to be just like You,
so I can love myself and then her.
Lord I want to become just like You,
so I can show her the "me" you intended for me to be,
so You can love me and I can learn how to love You.
Jesus as I become more like You,
I can become the right kind of me
so I can love my wife.
I want to become like Jesus
so I can love you as "my church" eternally.
I want to become the Shepherd to my flock!
I want to become Abraham to my Sarah,
so I can hear You when You knock
on my door and I will open it.
To let You in Jesus
and I will become You.
I will marry my wife
and she will become my church.
I will become all things to all people
so I can learn how to nurture
and only then will I be able to love you dearly.
When I become like Jesus I will always
want you near me.
I will protect you from all harm.
I will pray for and with you every day.
I will read the word to you
and hold you in my arms at night.
I will never let you go a day

without knowing you are loved right.
I will be the man of God you need me to be,
I will lead this family like it's supposed to be led.
I will take care of your every
spiritual, emotional, and physical need.
I will love you until the end of eternity.
I will lift you on a platform
where no one else can touch you but God and I.
And I will reside in this house with you forever…
Baby I am a changed man now,
I've become like Jesus,
and as I lay this flower on your casket
I promise to love you forever,
as you have loved me.
I will never let you go again.
I now understand what it means to love,
and it's all "because you first loved me."

© 2010 Robert T. Sells – all rights reserved

Karen "Kaye" Stackfield

    Karen "Kaye" (Smith) Stackfield (1964) grew up in Los Angeles, California. Her book reflects the joys and pains she experienced while growing up in South Central. The loss of her father at the tender age of 10, a mother unable to deal with reality, and two older siblings taken away from the family, left her with the responsibility of taking care of her younger siblings. Struggling to provide for the family, Karen took on babysitting jobs, ran errands for neighbors, and sometimes even shoplifted to make ends meet. On occasion, she and her younger sibling were forced to eat from the back of grocery stores to survive. When she got older, Karen worked at the corner market.

    All children have a strong desire to be loved, and Karen was no exception. However, her inexperience caused her to look for love in the wrong direction. As a result, her life experiences included drugs, sex, rape, heart break, and loss of friendships. She always believed in God, so no matter what happened, she would pray to God saying, "Haven't I been through enough? Can I get to know You now?" Much to her delight, she learned of a loving Creator who, through His Word the Bible, taught her to value herself and others, and how to love and even forgive those who had come in her path to this point.

In Karen's own words, "I want to be the friend you think of when you feel hurt or happy, or the friend you just want to talk about your day. I strive to be more loving and understanding to bridge the gap between you and your next goal. I love to help when I can, because there was a time in my life when everyone took from me and gave me no positive direction. I believe that if I had just one person to show me some positive direction, then I would have taken a different path. Today, I strive to be that person." Karen is now a wife of 26 years and the mother of two beautiful children.

WHY I WROTE:

The reason I'm participating is this anthology is because I'm a survivor of date rape, heart break, mental and emotional abuse and physical abuse. Domestic Violence affects not only the person involved but the entire family. If one person finds the courage to walk into a life free from abuse then I'm honored to share my story.

LINKS:
www.poeticrealities.com
Poeticrealities@gmail.com

In Search of a Better Life

I'm a red-bone girl of color searching for change, no longer the "blue jean queen," but the "sista" with a 9 to 5. Most of my co-workers don't look nor speak like me. I have been verbally, mentally and physically mistreated by my mother, which for a time left me with a void of self-esteem. So, at the age of sixteen I thought I would give love a chance, hoping to fill that void. Needless to say, what exactly would a sixteen year old know about love? My heart was broken twice at that age and the void was never filled. So I learned to protect myself by carrying a blade and selling drugs, which is not what I wanted to do with my life. That led me to my 9 to 5 job at an insurance company. My position there was file clerk.

Shortly after I started, this beautiful black man in a suit and tie walks in and notices me. It's not Sunday church, a wedding, or a funeral and yet he spoke so eloquently wearing his suit and tie. He sees me as fresh meat and I see him as round three in my quest for love and fulfilling my void of being in a relationship. We introduce ourselves and he invites me to a pool party at his place. I'm impressed that he has a pool. At that age I had never been to an apartment with a pool before. I hurried home after work so I could travel across town to the Westside, just to be in his presence. I purchased this new French cut bathing suit. I slide on my white sparkle dress, trying not to look sleazy and let's not forget my nude color leather candies. I stand 5'-2½, with measurements of 36-23-36 and I'm sexually active but just hoping for a kiss. Truth be told, I would have slept with him, just not on the first date. So, he picked me up in a nice car with soft jazz music playing. I was so intrigued, although R & B is my favorite music. I was looking for change and his jazz was mellow enough to be that change, except I was not ready to replace my R & B. We get to the party and the music was nice and the people were interesting and friendly. I had a really nice time. Once the party was over we headed back to his place and I took a seat on the couch while he went in his bedroom to change.

Suddenly he comes out of his bedroom undressed and attacks me. He rips my dress off aggressively while whispering, "You're so beautiful, you made me do this." He repeated this over and over again as he began to rape me. He has barely penetrated me and begins ejaculating. All the while he is repetitiously repeating the words, "You made me do this." I thought to myself, "Why did I ever stop carrying a blade?" All I wanted him to do was to kiss me. I thought he was a really nice man with a suit, however at this very moment I began hating myself for trusting him. He got dressed, took me home and thanked me for the evening. He even had the nerve to say, "I hope we can do this again." So for the next two years I hated myself. During those years and for some time after, every time someone told me I was fine or beautiful, I hated myself more.

Eventually, I quit my job and moved to San Diego, where I met a friend named Marshall. I told him I didn't want to go back to the city and he kindly offered me a place as his roommate. He was such a sweetheart. He never raised his voice at me and never tried to inappropriately touch me. This man was a true friend and stood beside me as I went through so many troubles. When I experienced mental flashbacks and would freeze in fear, he would always reassure me that I have moved past that painful period in my life. He confirmed for me that it was truly over. After two years of his kindness to me, I felt I had the love I needed to fill that void of being in a relationship and by Gods grace we were married.

Although my last 30 years have not been perfect, I have found true love in this man. I realize now that relationships are "works-in-progress" and I see that my husband loves me for who I was going to be, not for the broken young lady that I was. He loved me for being a friend, a loving mother and a trusted wife. This black man helped me see the benefits of being drug, alcohol, and profanity free. Within a year of having his last name, I realized that I had gone several days with being free of drugs, alcohol, and profanity for the first time since I was 12 years old. His hugs are so full of love, that to this day, I thank God for sending this man to me. This man took the time to learn my very breath and detect my sadness effortlessly and was willing to love me regardless. We share two beautiful children, and he leaves me thinking, "How can I love him more?"

Today my rape is like an old scar. I know it happened, but I rarely think of it unless asked. Through years of family turmoil, heart aches, and domestic violence, all of which I now call my stepping stones, I have found true love. I have learned to forgive my offenders because I realized if I did not portray forgiveness, it would eat at me like a cancer. I have chosen to retell my story, so those women that may have a similar experience can understand that hostile situations can get better. I had returned to being myself before the rape, before the first slap, before the abusive parent, mate, teacher, or counselor. We all have the ability to stand strong in our spirits and reach back to our inner beauty with help from God. Be the one to say I'm a SURVIVOR!

Just a Man

I'm a Man
that has burned many bridges,
as I have strived for three years to mend them,
I was in hopes that you would join me
as my wife and friend.

Your words cut so deeply
that at times they leave me numb,
With a pain so strong
I can't think…
Please know I only long to be loved,
not condemned.

The Beauty of Love is the Ability to Forgive

Love is my strongest quality.
The one I have always prayed to maintain
and struggled to hold on to.

No Matter what I face in life,
somehow love has brought me through.
The ability to forgive is the beauty of love.
To let go and start fresh is what we all long for;
when faced with our own errors.
May you forever possess the beauty of love…

A Mother's Greatest Pain

To see her child suffer needlessly
is a mother's greatest pain.
To hear her children cry,
yet, not be able to hold them,
and say it's okay.

My greatest pain
is to be separate from my children;
striving to make a better life for them,
knowing no one can ever love them like me.

Tamari Campbell

I was born in Springfield, Massachusetts. Through all of my struggles God has continued to be my guiding light. Without Him I would not be where I am today. I have been trying to write for years and never knew I could write as well as I do. I give many thanks to two very important people who encourage me to write poetry. These individuals are Kie Rodriguez and Tony Wade. I tapped into an amazing part of me and now poetry is a part of who I am. My goal is to release a poetry book sometime next year.

Tamari is currently in the process of working on her debut literary release. She is working to have her poetry book, "Pen to Paper" out by the end of 2011, with 2 more books to follow in 2012. For more on this talented poet, visit tamari on FB and view her web page.

LINKS:
www.tamaritoledo.weebly.com
www.facebook.com/tamari.toledo

Well, I guess I will start where I can remember.

This began when I was about three years old. I had the first abuse experience from my father. I was playing with my cousins on the first floor of our house. We lived on the third floor and my grandmother lived on the second floor. I asked my dad if I could take a bath at my aunt's house. Of course he said no, but I was three years old and went to my mom. We all know kids always try to get away with this one. If one parent says no, we'll try to get a yes from the other one.

Well, let's say it worked because my mom said yes and I was happy. I went down stairs and was in the tub when my dad comes in. He grabs me by the hair and drags me up to the third floor. All the while I'm screaming in pain and hiding behind my mom. I remember hearing my dad screaming, "If you don't get control of her she will become a tramp." Nice words, huh, especially when they are coming from your own father. Well, the abuse didn't stop there. I remember getting a lot of beatings from my dad. He would use belt buckles, shoes, extensions cords, hangers, plastic baseball bats; you name it, I got it. My dad was always saying, "Spare not the rod and spoil the child…"

That was drilled into me every day. There was no love in my home. My mom was nineteen when she had me, and my dad was living a double life. I was taken to all of the women's houses he was having an affair with. I was told that if I said anything to my mom I'd be killed. My mom was so focused on herself that she didn't have any time for me. No hugs, kisses or hearing the words "I love you." I was just there or at least I felt this way. I can't even remember how far back it was that I wanted to commit suicide. Everything I did was wrong! Then, at the age of seven, my dad tells me about my half brother and sister. I was so excited that I now had someone to talk to or so I thought. They hated me! I was the black sheep of the family and blamed as the cause of their mother Louise and my father's separation. Anyway, that is a long drawn out story that I will tell another day.

I was five years old when I was molested by my mother's cousin husband. He asked me to touch his penis and I did. What did I know at that age? I was confused and told it was a game. Then at age nine I was part of an orgy. As I got older I knew what it was. My first experience was with my cousin and a girl. Talk about having an identity crisis… Then the racial crisis! Think about being Black and Puerto Rican in a neighborhood filled with only black people. I was the only one going to a private school and yes that was a mess. I was getting beat on every day I got off the bus, because I didn't fit in on either side. I had no one to talk to, so I felt that my sexuality was normal. I just wanted love and for someone to care about me. Yes, I was called the project tramp. I joined a gang and my initiation was being raped by 14 boys in my neighborhood.

Was this ever going to get any better? My mom was no role model either. After she and my dad split she was out there like a cat in heat. But she doesn't remember these things, not even the things that I went through with both her and my father. I felt like my mom hated me. I remember taking a bottle of sleeping pills. I fought so hard to stay awake and not go to sleep. Luckily I did… I made it through making myself throw up. She woke up and asked me what was wrong. She was screaming and yelling because I wasn't ready for school. I told her I wanted to die and that I took a bottle of pills. It seemed like she didn't care. This is what I'm talking about. There was no love and understanding.

So once again I searched for love in all the wrong places. However, I did meet someone. He is my children's father. I met him when I was eleven years old. We talked on the phone for 2 years before we met. I fell madly in love with him but was in love with his voice. It is funny now but it wasn't back then. The first time we meet was through his front door window. We talked and got together. I made the first move. He was scared and told me to lose my virginity somewhere else before we slept together. You see, I wouldn't be his first but he would be mine. So I was on the course to sleep with someone and this guy from school, named Denny, was always after me. I finally gave in and he thought as well that he was my first. So off I went to my children's father. We slept together. I became pregnant at the age of thirteen. My daughter was born when I was 14 and the nightmare began. It wasn't with him beating on me but it was me beating on him. That's all I knew. I didn't know how to handle my anger. I would hit and bite him. He would never hit me back. I almost lost him. He took 10 years of abuse from me before he walked away and said no more. I stopped hitting him because he was the only one that truly loved me. But we only lasted 15 years together. His mother didn't want him to marry me, even though we had three kids together. I wasn't good enough for him; not Black enough for him as she put it. So our relationship ended.

I was going through a lot. My aunt, who was more like my mother, died on July 13th, 1997. That was two days after my birthday. She was the only woman who loved and cared for me unconditionally. No matter what I did in my life she held me and always told me she loved me. So when she passed away I was on destruction mode. I gave my daughter to my mom, and my two boys to their father. I wanted to be free and numb the pain, so party happy I became. I was breaking night while working and going to school. I wouldn't sleep for three or four days in a row. Then I meet the man of my dreams or so I thought. I received flowers at work every Friday. He brought me on expensive trips to New York City. After living all of my life in Massachusetts, I never experienced New York City the way he showed me. Eating lobster by the water, water boat rides, basically everything I never had he gave me. See, my children's father was an amazing man. Glenn worked his butt off 6 days a week. He wasn't a passionate or touchy kind of guy and not much for public displays of affection. But this guy I was in love with. He was so attentive to my needs. He hugged, held, kissed, and couldn't get enough of me.

So I was experiencing the hook line and sinker phase. However, 6 weeks in I received my first beating. I was black and blues all over the place. I had stopped dealing with my family, including my children, because he took me away from everyone. We made up, at least I thought, but it was a fluke! This couldn't be happening… I forgave him, but it just kept getting worse and worse. It got so bad that he terribly beat me in front of his mother. She called the cops and had him arrested. Yes, you would think after all of this that I was free of him, but no not me. I was working so much, but whatever spare time I had was used by visiting him while he was in jail.

He changed his ways tells me… He says he will never do it again… He's so sorry… He wants to marry me. So I wait until he gets out of jail and one week later we get married. I lost everything out in the streets. I lost my apartment and moved in with his mother. The beatings got worse and happened more often. I moved out his mother's house and into my grandmother's house. It was okay for a while but once I found my own place, it started all over again. One beating was so bad that I almost died. He hit me so hard that I hit my face on the corner of my bed post. The doctors told me that if my head had been struck 1 more centimeter higher on my temple, then I wouldn't be here today telling my story.

So here I am on the street again. He would spend my money. I was back putting my children into different places and being on the streets. This lasted until God answered my prayers. My abuser was caught trafficking drugs and sentenced to 7 years, 3 years in prison and 4 years on probation. But of course what do I decide do? You guessed it, I wait for him to be released and I try and save my marriage.

Yes, he came home. Not right away, but he did come home. The good man lasted about a month before it started all over again. But this time I was ready with no fear. I took my self worth back! He hit me and I hit him back. He yelled at me and I yelled back. I was not going to be the victim anymore! I was homeless three times because of him and going into a Domestic Violence shelter because of him motivated me to say and stand by the words, "Enough was enough!"

The last straw was when I found out about another affair he was having and I confronted him about it. Of course he denied it, but this time there were pictures and the jerk had the nerve to hit me because he got caught. Now can anyone explain to me how that works? He hit me so hard on the left side of my face that he perforated my left ear drum. That was it! I filed for divorce and called his parole officer and let him know what was going on. I saved his butt from going to jail for violating his restraining order and probation but I was tired of given up my tax dollars for him. He has a problem and if I can save the next woman from this I will.

So I thank Jah for all His help and getting me through this. With-out God I would not be where I am today. I am happy and free from this nightmare, once and for all!

G. P. A.

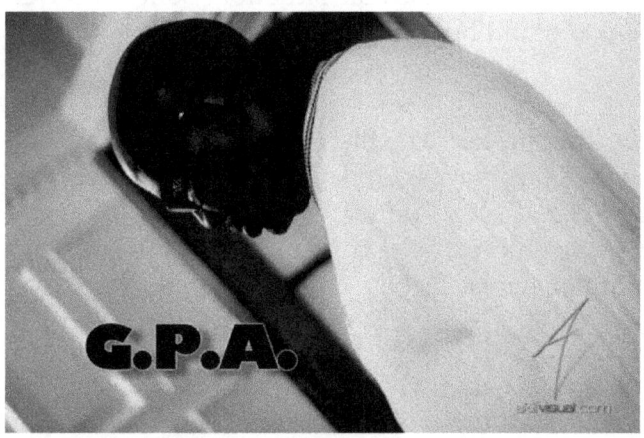

G.P.A. is from the south side of Chicago. He has been writing poetry since 2007 and published his first book of poetry, The Confessional Heart of a Man. He currently is a member of the Waiting for the Bus collective. G.P.A.'s website is www.iblowyourmind.com. He will be releasing his first cd of poetry "The GPA Experience" and the follow up to his first book, The Mind of an Unsub.

WHY I WROTE:

I abhor domestic violence. Every year I donate proceeds during the month of October towards a respective shelter or another. My reason for writing my poems and participating in this anthology is I have seen, been a victim, and falsely accused of domestic violence. And in each scenario, it was not a pleasurable situation. So it behooves me, for my part, to speak out and hopefully aid others.

LINKS:
www.facebook.com/gerald.pallen
www.facebook.com/pages/GPA-Greatest-Poet-Alive-Livingston/171281820040?ref=ts
twitter: gr8estpoetalive
youtube channel: hchise22

Dreamsnatcher

He told me I would never be shit,
my love was misguided and understand, so I believed it
Made it easier to rationalize and reconcile when i got hit
Pastor preached pathetic prayerful perseverance
After broken ribs, a broken arm, and two black eyes, my ears were no longer hearing.
For if I stayed one moment longer, then dead instead of battered is what I was fearing.
see I understood that times can be difficult in marriage
But we had two children,
but should've been three,
yet pregnancy aborted, by kicks to the stomach causing the miscarriage.
grabbed the kids, keys to my car, and the bank card with the mad money in a hidden bank account.
heart beating near out of my chest, racing against his arrival home, the tension mounts
Just then, he met me as I was rushing out the door!
Where do you think you're going because you're nothin' without me, you trifling, five dollar whore!
His fist swung and connected with my jaw.
Thankfully, that was the last time he would ever put his hands on me, last of him I ever saw.
Shots fired from the distance
His body bloodied by bullets fell with no resistance to the floor.
Son had tired of seeing his mother hurt; now there is a dream snatcher no more...

Unbelievable

Punches, kicks, slaps, things throughout the house used as wea-pons.
Dark skin hides the bruises upon my face
Embarrassed in front of family and friends
Harsh words, expletives, and negative reinforcement cause scars deep within
And at my constant consternation and subsequent sadness, abuser found reason to laugh and grin.
Think to call the police and put an end to this
But would they come?
Would they care?
Would they even believe me?
Perhaps they would take me in as the culprit, handcuff me, and charge me
Because I am a man...
So me being a victim of domestic violence would be
Unbelievable

Michele Tooles

Michele Tooles is a parent and Chicago native, who is finding her way in the literary industry. She is a stunning woman of sheer intelligence and is the host of her own online radio talk show on BlogTalkRadio, where she is provocative and infuriating. To date, she has over 30 years of experience in using her brain and speaking her mind. She holds no punches and is very candid and at times brash in her commentary of current events and social issues. She prides herself on being genuine and not an expert. Her literary venture is taking off, as she has established a reading club and is working on promoting authors under her alter ego, Ms. Daring of The Daring Show.

WHY I WROTE:

I actually have a couple of reasons for wanting to participate in this anthology. First, thank you for the opportunity to express myself on this topic. Second, we have all been touched by the effects of Domestic Violence. I am no exception to this; I have had family and friends that received this treatment. My writings look at things from a segued and angled approach of the person on the outside looking in, as opposed to the abuser or the abused. I think it's important we acknowledge those that are looking in, that don't know what to do or how to do anything, because the whole incident affects them psychologically as well. Violence doesn't just stay in that person's house. The mindset and attitude permeate the eyes, ears and lives of all those in the vicinity. The other reason I would like to participate is to leave a legacy for my man-child, that there is nothing we do that doesn't have a direct or indirect influence over another.

LINKS:
Email: thedaringshow@gmail.com
Radio Show: www.blogtalkradio.com/thedaringshow
Website: www.thedaringshow.blogspot.com

Voices Behind the Tears

Excerpt from upcoming novel

Slap!!!

"Ooouch", the moan and groan continued. She was hit, with no afterthought and all malice. How could she have been so stupid, she thought.

"SHUT THE FUCK UP," shoving her to the floor. She hit her shoulder on her way down against the side of the coffee table.

Crack!!

"Ahhhhhhhhhhh…" Tears franticly leave her eyes, as if they are in search of help. "Please stop, I'm sorry," she begged, as her broken shoulder gave her grave agony.

He stood over her cowering body and authoritatively said, "You are one stupid bitch! Didn't I tell you to be here by 5:30?"

Yelling in pain and despair, "I'M So-r-r-y," while emphatically crying. She just wanted him to stop, leave, and even go to hell. She just wanted him to get the farthest away from her.

"You right you're sorry," he said, while scoffing at her pathetic sight balled up on the floor.

Kicking her legs he yelled, "Get up and clean yourself up. I'm going home! You fucked up what was almost a nice evening."

Mr. turned and walked out the house.

Lea just cried and cried. What lie could she tell people about what happened to her? How was she going to get away from him? How did she get into this?

Shaking her head she realized that the first thing she had to do was go and get her shoulder looked at.

One day a friend asked me to talk to a woman he knew about the violent relationship she is a part of. With me being the harsh individual I can be from time to time, I immediately started to give my personal opinion on the subject. However, I realized that I could not provide help to the issue but only add further degradation to the situation. So after constantly tapping the backspace and delete keys, I decided to type some of my more mild viewpoints down, to attempt to expound on my perspective, in an attempt to clarify my disdain for this activity and any agreement of such behavior.

Because this is a delicate subject, it requires that those who choose to address it use plain English and calm tones. I don't know why just then, I thought I was talking about paint, but I digress. I do have a problem with being calm but this will be my best attempt at it. You may not agree or like my opinion but it is mine and I am entitled to it, as are you. So here we go.

One in four women (25%) has experienced domestic violence in her lifetime.
Nearly three out of four (74%) of Americans personally know someone who is or has been a victim of domestic violence...
(Facts provided by:
http://www.dvrc-or.org/domestic/violence/resources/C61/)

Every 9 seconds in the US a woman is assaulted or beaten. Studies suggest that up to 10 million children witness some form of domestic violence annually. Domestic violence victims lose nearly 8 million days of paid work per year in the US alone — the equivalent of 32,000 full-time jobs...
(Facts provided by: http://domesticviolencestatistics.org/domestic-violence-statistics/)

Violence by an intimate partner accounts for about 21% of violent crime experienced by women and about 2 % of the violence experienced by men. 31,260 women were murdered by an intimate from 1976-1996...
(Facts provided by: http://www.aardvarc.org/dv/statistics.shtml)

Too much domestic assault is happening lately and I'm really getting tired of hearing the stories as they get more tragically dramatic. For those putting their hands on a person in a sense of brutality, because they aren't woman or man enough to deal with their aggressive nature is a sign of an enormously insignificant person.

I mean really, how intelligent do you have to be to throw a punch? How responsive can a person be after receiving a blow to their face, mouth, abdomen, kidneys? How about a shoe impression to their skull or gurgling on their own blood? Yes cringe, which is what you need to do. I want you to think of the horrific pain and torture someone experiences as they are getting dragged around the house by their hair. What feeling do you get thinking of the woman who is getting her head bashed in on the wall or floor while her child watches in horror and the only words he/she can scream is "MOMMA"? Oh, I have more stories that I could vividly detail but I think you get the picture. And it's not pretty is it?

It is not pretty, it is not healthy, it is morally and psychologically unsound to let someone do that to you or to be the abuser. Even though I listed statistics on domestic violence, it is a waste of valuable time telling that information to a victim. Telling them about the social ramifications of accepting that type of treatment is a mute point. Would it give you incentive to remove yourself from that type of situation when hearing about those that didn't make it? All the statistics look bleak; they don't show the positive side of anything. As per the statistics she will be dead by the end of the year. Is that the message you really want to hear or reveal to someone in that position?

Exactly! It doesn't seem too effective. Although there are no easy words or ways to address this concern with the person/people you are trying to help, you can start by understanding the sickness. Some victims feel it is love and their fault or they cannot do any better in a partner. As the outsider you can tell them that the offender that assaulted them is a thief and a murderer. That individual has stolen the dimly lit light that was within their loved ones soul and murdered the confidence and trust that they bestowed to them in return for a stable, safe and healthy relationship.

Abused victims, especially those that have stayed in a situation for a long period of time, need to go through the steps of grief and to understand that to them, they should be the most important thing on this planet. They need to know that they are worthy, loved and that they have the ability to conquer all adversities.

Healing starts within and those that wish to help need to focus on rehabbing this dilapidated building and making it feel like a skyscraper. Seek shelter, family, a group, a lawyer (not necessarily in that order).

Life is too short and the perpetrator does not mean any good to anybody and we all can do badly by ourselves.

The thieving executioner has low self-esteem and cannot be fixed without professional assistance. Get out, run out and take the only possessions worth saving yourself and your children and do not look back. He is not worth it. This violence happens to men also. I did not really ignore you but for the sake of space I had to focus. The LGBT community is not exempt from this problem and therefore the same applies, GET SOME HELP ASAP (and that doesn't stand for "always say a prayer" either)!!!

National Domestic Violence Hotline at

1-800-799-SAFE (7233)
Or TTY 1-800-787-3224

http://www.thehotline.org/
Domestic Violence Awareness Month is in October.

Elizabeth Funderbirk

**Why I started "Saving Lives Through Lit"
and why I wanted to write.**

    The idea to write a story centered on Domestic Violence came from an Internet radio show that I was listening to. Hearing someone else speak their truth made me want to share a story I knew needed to be told. However, in the process of writing, I became hesitant. I reached out to Kiexiza and explained to her my idea to start an anthology. The purpose is to give a voice to those who are still hesitant to reach out and ask for HELP. I wanted the profits to be used for donations to charities that will aid Domestic Violence Victims. I believe in the power of numbers. So, to make this a collection of various stories that would speak about Domestic Violence and all the emotions that come from dealing or witnessing it, was a comfort to me. I would be amongst others who also needed to release a story inside of them. That is what I want for the people who that purchase "Voices Behind the Tears." I want them to know that they are not alone in this struggle. I want them to feel comforted by the stories that are similar to theirs and to be uplifted and know that there is a LIFE beyond the battle of Domestic Violence. Making this a project based on donations and volunteered services, from writers, editors, and various literary talents, who gave selflessly of their time, talent, and efforts which further cemented that this was a book and movement that was in NEED.

We want charities and organizations that have dedicated them-selves to the cause to partner with "Saving Lives Through Lit" to raise funds for the women, men, and children in need. Fundraising is not a new concept. What "Saving Lives Through Lit" provides is a new outlook and another way to reach the public. Using a literary twist to raise funds promotes literacy, as well as giving the purchaser a book; they will forever have a copy as a show of their donation and assistance to those who need it. The victim who purchases this book will forever have a collection of stories, poems, and notes in their possession when their voice is not strong enough to reach out for help. They will be able to read "Voices Behind the Tears" and find solace. I hope you can share in my joy of knowing that a portion of the funds generated from this anthology will help another woman, man and child face the same crossroads.

I wrote my story to release what was on my heart and soul. I wrote my story to help those in turmoil. I wrote my story because I want my writing to be about a purpose.

BIO:
Elizabeth is mother, wife, writer, blogger, business woman, sister, friend, daughter, and survivor. Originally from New York City, NY, Liz moved to Buffalo, NY at a young age. Although she has lived in several states over her 31 years of life, she now calls Myrtle Beach, South Carolina home.

She began her writing career as a blogger of the Literary Journal "Trials, Tribulations, and Torn" in 2009. This is a journal of her journey to becoming a published author. This also follows the trials she faced in her personal life, as well as the journey of trying to navigate her way through an industry she knew little to nothing about.

Since then her blog has grown leaps and bounds and she is always working to keep it up-to-date. Several of her articles and posts ranked 1-6 on the Google search. The top ones are "Publishing a Body of Work" and "What happens after You have Finished Writing your Manuscript?"

Elizabeth Funderbirk's debut Novel, "Love TORN Asunder", is a relationship drama that is available online through all major book retailers and also on Kindle, Nook, and all E-readers. The second book of this four book series is scheduled to be released in the Fall/Winter 2011.

She has contributed articles to other Blogs and Web Magazines. Her poetry and official debut book review can be found in Mattie's Periodicals, which is a quarterly literary publication.

She is the owner of a start up web design firm, which specializes in affordable web sites that are built by templates. EyeDesign4u Solutions motto is "Allow us."

Elizabeth is also one of the founders of "Saving Lives Through Lit" along with Kiexiza Rodriguez, and serves as the President.

LINKS:
Literary Liz writes: http://LiteraryLiz.com
Trials, Tribulations, & Torn: http://writingtorn.blogspot.com
EyeDesign4u Solutions: http://www.wix.com/literaryliz/eyedesign
Saving Lives Through Lit:
http://www.savinglivesthroughlit.org/founders
Emerald Star Press www.Emeraldstarpress.net

Praying For A Dream- Short Story By: Elizabeth Funderbirk

The Anticipation

It's so soft and quiet but my senses are heightened and the blades from the ceiling fan whirling above me, in a never ending rotation, sound more like a chopper flying through the heavy night air. The warm breeze from the spinning fan does little to dry the sweat from my damp skin. Even as I lay here still, my breath is coming in spurts and sweat continues to drain from my pores.

I know he is not done. He never comes for a quick visit. I smell his stench as he makes his way towards me. Even before he makes it inside the room, I smell the combination of sweat, alcohol and piss.

I can hear the thud of his workman boots coming down the car-peted hallway. The steps are slow and deliberate. It's as if he knows the sound alone makes me soil myself right there on my mattress. That will not stop his assault though. Nothing ever did. Then the sound of the jingle of his belt buckle being undone alerts me of how close he is. I close my eyes and I can see him undoing his belt as the clanking sound grows louder with each thud from his steps. He's here! The door knob twists and the sting between my legs begins to throb in anticipation for what he has in store next. I wonder if I will survive it this time. Will this be his final visit? Will my passing out into a never ending sleep cease his pursuit?

I no longer have the will to fight. He beat my ability to run out of me a long time ago. He fucked my self-respect out of my soul with each violent thrust of his powerful heavy manhood.

A New Day

The images usually fade with the rise of the sun. This time was different. This time I'm afraid that his secret, which happens to be my shame, will not be hidden behind a closed door, drawn curtains, and sealed lips.

I am far from the typical high school student. I work hard to keep inquiring minds out of my personal life. It's not easy though when your best friend is constantly questioning you about your state of mind. Did she suspect something? I thought that I wanted to shed my skin and bare my truth but now that it seemed like she may be questioning my actions, I felt too exposed and wanted to hide in my shame. Hide quietly in my personal agony. My misery was not longing for company.

I lied to keep the question at bay. I have been living a lie so long I was not sure if I even knew the truth anymore.

House of Horrors-

The walk leading to my door was similar to walking the plank. I felt like once I cross the threshold to my house I would be lost in the never ending abyss, similar to those that drown at sea. Unlike them, I did not get the satisfaction of choking until death came to greet me. I was held prisoner by the night and instead of the sweet release of life leaving my body, I was being consistently and deliberately strangled; in an agonizingly slow manner.

The door swung open slowly and even held a creek, like the sounds found in scary movies. It would have been amusing if I didn't live in a real life house of horrors. Silence was on the other side of the door to greet me and for the first time today I was able to breathe. I took to the stairs and rushed into the bathroom. I had no idea when the other people whom I live with would return, so I had to be quick. Knowing my family, the phase was laughable. No one in this house acted as a family anymore. We co-existed. I locked the door behind me and hurriedly stripped myself and hopped into the shower. No matter how many times I bathed in water hot enough to boil my skin, that scent, his scent, was now permanently on me. The thought of him caused me to go into hyper speed. I needed to hurry and make it back to my room. Not that the closed locked doors ever stopped his pursuit, but if I could just get enough time to myself to think…

I press my face to the wooden rickety door and listen intently. I'm waiting to hear footsteps, voices, his breathing, belt buckle, anything. I even get down on my hands and sore knees and look out the slit between the door and floor, and inhale. I smell for the scent that is seared into my memory to see if I see shadows. Almost as if, in fearful anticipation, I was waiting for his feet to greet me. But there was nothing! For the second time today my lungs fill completely with oxygen and I am able to exhale.

I run to my bedroom door. As soon I close it behind me the images take form. I see him and I am his prisoner. I'm jumping into my sweats and sit in the corner with no lights turned on, curtain drawn, and begin to write. That is the only time I can really express myself. This is the only time I can say what I really feel and there will be no looks of shame cast upon me. My journal has become my life jacket. While I float away in the direction of insanity, my journal is what keeps me anchored.

The Great Escape-

When I write I am able to escape into my mind. I always visit the same time and place. It's so familiar to me yet the safety of it is so far away.

I remember waking up on my 5th Birthday. That was one of the happiest days in my life. That was when my mother loved me. She cared for me. She was my protector. She was truly my everything. I was so happy to wake up on that April day that I think I floated out the bed and skipped through the hallways. I remember my house being filled with light. The sun rays were steaming through every window. The smell of a clean breezed through the house. It was on this day that I could always reach back to and reflect upon a moment of happiness. I ran into my mother's room and she laid there under her covers. I knew she was pretending to be asleep. As soon I got close she would toss the cover back and grabbed me. She covered me with the sweetest kisses. She hugged me tight as if I was the reason why she lived. She would always smell the space between my neck and chin. Then she would kiss it with a big wet sloppy kiss. She knew that I was so ticklish there and I would fall out laughing. She said that was my sweet spot. She said that out of all the places she kissed me, that spot was definitely the sweetest.

I gaze at my belongings and my twin size bed. It had Strawberry Shortcake sheets and a matching comforter and pillow case that topped it all off. I received it on my 5th birthday. I remember wanting to make my bed right away. With my mother by my side, together we dressed my bed and I slid beneath the tightly made blankets and rolled around.

However, that beautiful day of spending quality time with my mother transformed into a fading memory. It became faded and tattered like the strawberry shortcake sheets that remain on my bed to this day. The years changed after that. The climate in my once warm, sun filled home became dark, and sullen. I sit in the corner of this room that I have out grown and wonder what happened to the room that I played in that was more like a castle. It once had room for me, friends, and laughter. I feel small in this space now. My once castle is now my coffin.

The Harsh Reality-

A rapt knock on my door bring fear of the present. I am no longer in my dreamland of a five year old in her castle. I am a scared sixteen year old huddled in the corner of her bedroom. The knock comes again and reminds me that if I don't answer the consequences can be unbearable. If you can, imagine that feeling of despair.

The voice on the other side was not who I was expecting. She fidgeted as she spoke, as if she didn't know what the right thing to say to me anymore was. I lied to avoid having to look at her or continue this meaningless banter. She sounded relieved that I was avoiding her. I was relieved that her small footsteps carried her away from my door without pressing the issue. I remain rooted in my spot and listen to her bedroom door creak open and softly close shut. Then I hear the locks seal my mother in and me out.

Praying For A Dream-

His last visit was just as violent and degrading as all the rest. However, he did something that I was not prepared for. He usually pulled out and sprayed his foul cum all over my face and forced me to lick it up. Last night he didn't. He allowed his seeds to ooze inside of me. The possibility that life could be created from this ungodly union scared me. It scared me more than the sound of his boots approaching, his belt buckle loosening, and the rattle of the door knob before he entered.

I needed to get to my happy place. This place came alive when I closed my eyes tight and wished the images away. However, the images prevailed. The freighting thoughts of a baby growing inside me had me on edge. I prayed that when my eyes closed I could be that five year old again.

I rolled over onto my side and took out a tiny bottle. This was a sleep aid prescribed to my mother for depression. I stared at the title, Ramelteon, through the darkness. I tried to focus on the words but thoughts of what it would be like to be that little girl forever danced inside my mind. What if I could fall asleep and always be in the place on that day? Before I knew it I had emptied the contents of the tiny bottle into my womb. Was I ready to give birth to a child? How could I bring a baby into this house to suffer the same fate that I have? I decided I wouldn't.

With no water to chase it down, I swallowed over and over to get every pill down. The dryness of my mouth made it easy for me to count as each pill entered my throat, traveled through my esophagus, and reached their final resting place in my stomach. Once I had counted 47. I closed my eyes again. This time my prayer was asking God to forgive me for whatever sin I surely committed. I found myself in an awful predicament.

I lay still in the night and the only sound I hear is the beat of my heart. It was abnormally rapid. I felt like it was threatening to burst my chest open. "Ba-Boom... Ba-Boom... Ba-Boom... Ba-Boom..." Then it eased and slowed. I flash through my short life span of sixteen years and so many of my memories are tainted. "Ba-Boom... Ba-Boom... Ba-Boom..." This is the sound of my slowing pulse lulling me deeper into my subconscious. "Ba-Boom... Ba-Boom... "She was hazy but I could still make her out. It was me. I was happy. I was five. The world was happy and life was good. "Ba-Boom... Ba-Boom..." My breaths are heavy, slow, and deep. They are releasing fewer and fewer. The more space between my labored breaths and the clearer she became. "Ba-Boom..."

I remember waking up on my 5th Birthday. That was one of the happiest days in my life. That was when my mother loved me. She cared for me. She was my protector. She was truly my everything. I was so happy to wake up on that April day that I think I floated out the bed and skipped through the hallways. I remember my house being filled with light. The sun rays were steaming through every window. The smell of a clean breezed through the house. It was on this day that I could always reach back to and reflect upon a moment of happiness. I ran into my mother's room and she laid there under her covers. I knew she was pretending to be asleep. As soon I got close she would toss the cover back and grabbed me. She covered me with the sweetest kisses. She hugged me tight as if I was the reason why she lived. She would always smell the space between my neck and chin. Then she would kiss it with a big wet sloppy kiss. She knew that I was so ticklish there and I would fall out laughing. She said that was my sweet spot. She said that out of all the places she kissed me, that spot was definitely the sweetest.

My prayers have been answered... I am drifting away on the day of my dreams. I will forever be happy within this day.

Luna Charles

Luna Charles is a self-publish author and the Director of Hardcastle Enterprises Corp., a business dedicated to helping those who are ready to realize the full potential that they have within. As the oldest of 5 kids from a single mother, Luna learned early that life may not seems fair but hard work and dedication will get you to where you want to go. Daily in her work, she strives for excellence using those early lessons to reinforce her spirit and those around her when times get tough. Her first novel Men Are Not The Problem is a heartfelt story of overcoming adversity and finding the love within which can conquer all wounds. Along with writing, Luna spends her time speaking to the youth in her local Florida community, raising her two daughters and spending time with her husband. She is currently working on a journal due out later on this year. Luna is Haitian by birth but has lived in South Florida for the last 21 years of her life.

WHY I WROTE:

As a child in Haiti, my life was constantly touched by violence, though not domestic. The memories of death, destruction and pain still fill my heart with pain and trepidation for all those who still live under those circumstances.

At 12 years old my step father raised his hand to my mother. I cowered in the corner with my baby sister and youngest brother. I was too afraid to move because of a past I had left behind. My other little brother went at his dad with all the power that his little seven year old fist could muster. My mother, being a woman of insurmountable mental strength, quickly taught her husband that - that night would be the first and last time he would ever touch her like that in front of her children.

My mother was extremely lucky compared to other women who faced similar circumstances.

Today, too many stories are heard and told every day, hour, and minute that involve someone being hurt by somebody whom they loved and trusted. Too many women feel like they do not have a way out; that they somehow deserve to be treated less than the divine creation of the Universe that they truly are. My hope, is that I at least inspire one, to take a step forward towards a better tomorrow with my words.

LINKS:
www.lunacharles.com
luna@lunacharles.com
twitter.com/luna_charles
facebook.com/lunacharles
menarenottheproblem.com

Mommy's Little Girl

"Right now I don't know who you are. You are a stranger to me. Look at you, you're drunk! Who the hell gave you alcohol?" My mother was yelling at me. We were standing in the hallway between the kitchen and the dining room. She had come home from some VA organization meeting to find me passed out drunk at the dining room table on a school day.

I was so tired of her yelling at me. It was as if I could not do any-thing right. Everyone at school either made fun of me or pitied me as the half breed whose dad died in the war. Then I would come home to find her drunk and crying, wishing she had stopped him from doing that second tour. Most of the time I felt like I was screaming for help in a room full of people and no one cared to listen. I was so frustrated and angry.

"No one gave it to me mom. I stole it out of your fucking stash!" I shouted at her.

Somewhere inside I knew I should not speak to my mother that way. That is not how I was raised. But I didn't care anymore. I had made up my mind that she didn't care about me. That whatever love she and I shared died with dad on the battlefield. Now all we were was two carcasses, empty of life, doomed to live in this hell, physically together but emotionally apart.

Smack! It was the sound of flesh hitting flesh.

Her hand hit the tender meat of my face with such speed that it had clearly returned to her side before I felt it. I stood there in shock for a minute. My palm caressing my now inflamed cheek. She looked as stunned as I felt hurt. Yet the pain was transforming into rage faster that I could control it. My whole 5'9" frame moved forward and grab her by her petite shoulders. I thought for a moment I saw her face transformed into shock and disbelief. But the emotional reaction that I should have had over my mother's response was overcome by the malice in my mind. Somewhere inside I think my heart cried that this was not happening again. That this was not something it thought my body was capable of, that this person shaking her mother was not Natasha. Yet I ventured on with this course of action.

"What the fuck is your problem?" I screamed at my mother as I shook her violently.

"Natasha, stop!"

I heard her but I could not stop.

"You've been drinking every day since dad died!" I slapped her, "You left me in this miserable, cold, desolated state to deal with this shit all by myself, while you hide your feelings." I screamed.

"Tash, Jesus, what's gotten into you? You're hurting me. What the hell." She shouted…

"Fuck you Mom!" I screamed, as I fisted my hand and hit her across the face.

She fell onto the wooden floor, a heap of jeans and fitted business shirts. She looked up at me in fear as disbelief marked her face. It had been the same look that I saw when I had walked into the house that day we found out about dad. There my mother had stood with the folded flag against her breast, as Sergeant White comforted her as best he could. All those feelings of lost, pain and disbelief came rushing back. I kicked her hard in the stomach. She screamed out. But I could not stop. Tears blurred my visions. I fell on top of her, rage over coming any sense that I had left. I lifted my hands over my head ready to strike her again, but before I could land another blow, she grabbed my hands in an attempt to defend, rolling her body from under me. Sooner than I knew what was happening, she had let go of my left arm and had my right hand twisted behind my back as she forced my face to the floor.

"Get off of me," I kept screaming. "It's all your fault he's dead. You let him go. You should have told him to stay. You should have…"

"Tasha, it's no one's fault except the bastard that killed your dad. We talked about this in counseling."

"I hate you!" I screamed…

"You're drunk!" she countered. Sitting back, she moved to grab the other arm, but quickly let go when she saw what I had been hiding under the long sleeves.

"You're cutting yourself again!" She attempted to scream, but her voice broke half way through as she started crying.

Getting off of me, she moved to the dining room and sat in one of the cherry wood chairs. I turned my body over from my place on the floor, with all the fight gone from me. Now I felt shame for having lost my temper and hitting my mother again. I was such a disgrace, so stupid. No wonder dad had taken another tour assignment. No wonder he would rather be fighting than be home with me. I looked up at my mom. She just sat there crying into her hands. Her blonde hair had fallen in disarray on the table top.

"Baby girl, I love you so much, so fucking much. You're all that I have left in this world. Please tell me what is happening to you, tell me what to do?" She asks in between sobs.

"You can't help me mom. You can't." I stood up and moved towards the back door, next to the table. She stood up so fast that the chair fell with thud behind her. She grabbed me. I flinched from the pain. She moved in between me and the door. Her cheek was swollen and bright red. In a few hours the bruise would turn a nasty purple color. I could not stand to see what I had done to her. I started crying harder.

"I just want to die mom. I just want it all to end. I can't do anything right." I fell to the floor and wrapped my arms around myself, pulling my sweaters sleeves over the palm of my hands, hiding the carnage that I had inflicted on myself below them. She sat on the floor with me, pulling me into her arms. Stroking my long dirty blonde curls, she sat there and cried with me.

This was not my first outburst. In fact, it was my second outburst that involved me hitting my mother. The first had been 2 years ago, after dad died. I had never liked living in Northern Michigan. It was too cold and I was one of the few black kids at school, although the other black kids didn't consider me one of them since I was mixed. Dad had been my support. He had faced discrimination in his life. But mom didn't know what it was like to be an outcast; not really belonging to any group. She was perfect in every way. How could she possibly understand me? How could she sympathize with me about being too tall to date? How could she even understand that the rich kids who looked more like her than I did all made fun of me and called me half breed? How could she see that I stopped feeling anything after dad died?

That's why I started cutting myself. The pain was a welcome deviation from the emptiness inside. Each time I took a razor blade and put it against my arm I would think to myself, if I was just strong enough to press it down a little harder, just a little deeper, just a little bit farther down my arm against my wrist, it would all be over. But I knew my father would never forgive me so I started sneaking drinks. My mom was so busy with the bills and life without my dad that she didn't even notice until I got into a fight with one of the cheerleaders.

The principal called my mom and told her that I had showed up at school drunk. She hadn't even listened to my side of the story. Instead, we drove home in absolute silence. As soon as we had walked into the house she started yelling at me and punishing me. I was so mad that had I hit her and kept hitting her until she slammed me into a wall.

The next day we were sitting in Dr. Rodriguez's office. My mom was complaining to the counselor about how she doesn't know what to do with me anymore. Dr. Rodriguez had listened intently to my mother before asking what was going on with me. When I started to speak, Dr. Rodriguez, who had been intently staring at my arms the whole time we were there, suddenly interrupted. He asked why I was wearing such a long sweater during one of the warmest days in Michigan's history. I remember how that question had startled my mom. How she had reached over and grabbed my arm, pulling the sweater up, exposing the cuts for all to see. How her whole face had contoured into pure pain, as if she had been punched in the guts by a sledge hammer when she saw them.

Now 2 years later here we were, on the floor, her begging me to let her in, me not knowing how.

"I had sex with this guy," I started out. She didn't say anything, she just held me tighter as she caressed my hair. "I thought he really liked me. We skipped school and went to his house. I had too much to drink and fell asleep after. He took pictures of me and passed them around the school." I started crying harder.

"I hate it here mom. Why can't we move? I know you want to stay because this was the last place you and dad were together, but every year we are here is another year that I want to die." Hearing those words she pulled me closer.

"Mom, please…" I continued.

She didn't say anything. Both my grandmother's had begged her to move back to Florida where her and my dad had met, and most of our family was. But she wouldn't have it. This was the last place dad had been she argued. She thought this house still had a piece of him inside of it. I on the other hand didn't feel the same. This house only reminded me that we were no longer whole. No matter how long I sat in front of the big picture window, I knew that he wouldn't be walking up the walkway in his army fatigues ever again. She just continued to hold me and cry.

Finally she spoke.

"We need help. And it's more help than I think I am able to give you on my own. You can't keep letting things build up inside of you until you hurt yourself and me. I thought Dr. Rodriguez had helped us. I thought that you knew you could talk to me. But, I guess I've been so busy hiding my own feelings and fears about you growing up without a dad, that I didn't notice that you are growing up without a mom either. I'm so sorry Tasha baby. I know you hate the house and the school. I know you want to move. At first I wanted to stay because of the memories of your dad, but now I see that you are the most important part of your dad that I still have and I'm destroying you by staying." She pulled me away from her and held me by the shoulders at arm's length.

"Let's seriously talk about moving. Grandma Jackson is always sending houses for sale emails of places in her area and she's not too far from my mom. We will get through this. I love you."

I opened my eyes to look at her. I saw the bruise on her face and started crying.

"I'm so sorry mom, so sorry." I cried as I fell back into her arms unable to look at her face. "I don't deserve to live. I'm nothing but some half breed slut. I hate myself so much."

"Shush baby, shush… you're a wonderful, beautiful, young woman. You are not a slut, that guy was an ass! You deserve better than that. If you want I will talk to his mom about the photos. I will threaten to have him arrested and you can be home schooled until we have everything settled for the move. I will not lose you. Tell me what you want me to do to make things better?"

I had no answer to her question. In my heart all I really needed was her. We had spent the last 2 years in counseling talking to each other but not listening. Each of us was lost in our own pain.

"Momma, I'm so sorry for hitting you. I know I'm angry at you because I feel like you're not there for me and that I am all alone to deal with everything. But that is no reason for me to ever touch you. Inside I'm so lost momma, so lost…"

"Shush, its okay baby. I'm lost too. I haven't known which way I've been going since that day Sergeant White came here. It's okay. We may not be the three musketeers anymore but we still have each other and we will find a way back to a place of happiness."

We sat there on the floor for a while. It was like the last 2 years of counseling had culminated to this event. For the first time I felt like my mother and I were listening to each other. I let my pain and fear go and just allowed her to hold me like she use to when dad was away and I had a nightmare. His loss had placed an invisible wall between us, but now I felt like that wall was crumbling. I knew I had a problem and now I felt like my mom had finally felt my pain and would help me. Finally I got up and helped my mom to my dad's leather recliner. I ran to the kitchen and grabbed some ice for her face. I apologized again as I sat on the floor at her feet.

"Everything is going to be okay." She repeated these words and for once I believed her.

I had wronged my mother in the most awful way, but I vowed I would make it better. I would make her proud.

The next day she called the school and advised them that we would be moving and that I would be home schooled until then. She called my grandmother on speaker phone and told her we wanted to move back. My grandmother cried when she heard that, and so did I. Finally, after so long, I felt like there was hope for our relationship again. I guess all I ever wanted was for her to listen.

Carlet Horne

Carlet Horne, an Honor Graduate of Whiteville High School, attended New York University and Southeastern Community College, while studying Business Administration and Education. Although her very first piece was written in 2008, she, thinking this was just a one-time occurrence, put her pen and pad on the shelf. In 2010, in the timing of God, the gift within her was unlocked, and she began to write under the unction of God. "My writing has been used as a source of healing and recovery from hurts, wounds, and issues of my past and I pray that the same is true for those who read any of my work," states Ms. Horne. Today, she is a Poet, Writer, and aspiring Author, working on the publication of her first book of Christian poetry and a contributing poetry writer for Promoting Purpose Magazine. Other examples of her work can be seen on www.TimBookTu.com and in Black Pearls Magazine and Inspired Women Magazine.

WHY I WROTE:

First and foremost, Domestic Violence in and of itself is simply... WRONG! To be able to shed light, in some form, on something as dark as this is the reason I chose to participate. I have seen the aftermath of events related to Domestic Violence, and its affects can be long-reaching. If something that I write changes someone's life for the better, then my mission in this will have been accomplished.

LINKS:
gfmember2005@hotmail.com
chorne11@facebook.com
http://facebook.com/chorne11
www.AsHeSpeaks.weebly.com
chorne@ashespeaks.weebly.com
www.facebook.com/chorne11

Voices Behind the Tears

"**My Name is....D.V.**"

Hello to you all
My name is D.V.
I'm not the latest Television Star
Or Rap Celebrity

Yet I'm internationally known
But I'm locally born and bred
My reach and influence
Are both far and widespread

"Who am I?" You ask
Let me give you a clue
Just in a case I stop by
And try to visit you

I may start out talking nice and very sweet
Then for no reason my voice escalates, reaching its peak
It's nothing you've said or done
It's something inside I must overcome

My internal rage rises
Fueled by an unsuspecting external cause
I try my best to maintain
And keep it inside neatly contained

But as luck would have it
My boiling point I reach
And to One I claim to love
A lesson I must teach

I may start with a grab
A slap or a smack
I usually take one's power
Leaving them no room to fight back

Saving Lives Through Lit

If I ever strike out
To the capacity of my rage
Someone will be left
In a battered and bruised stage

The results may prove fatal
Even leading to death
Which could have been avoided…
If I had stepped back and taken a breath

You asked before, "Who am I?"
I'm D.V.; Domestic Violence is my name
I'm a real part of someone's everyday life
And trust me, it's no game

The way to get rid of me
Starts during one's youth
Teach Core Life Values; Have loving relationships
And in Wisdom always teach the Truth

And if I am, by chance
A part of your everyday life
Give me the boot and kick me out
You deserve to live free from my wrath and strife

My Name is D.V. and I approve this message!

Voices Behind the Tears

<u>NO....</u>

The word...NO
Is a two-letter word loaded with Power
When spoken with authority
They stand as a strong tower

NO one has the right
To invade your personal space
"Stay eighteen inches away' was once taught
To avoid getting in another's face

NO one has the right
To touch another inappropriately
"Keep your hands to yourself" was the Golden Rule
And it's the way it should still be

Whether it's a friendly tap
Between two at play
When one says....NO
Take your hands away

NO one has the right
To put their hands on you
Whether in love or in anger
When you say NO, Stop is what they must do

Be clear and concise
Say it loud and proud
Let your NO be NO
Whether alone or in a crowd

Domestic Violence is real
It robs and steals
And for some
It even kills

It takes from not only its victim

Saving Lives Through Lit

But the family and even the offender
Takes away time, money, and security
Things that were once your dependents

The charge could start as Simple Assault
From violating a Fifty (50) B
Then in front of the judge you stand
For him to make a decree

It all depends on what took place
When the police arrive at the space
But for a ride in the backseat someone will go
All because they wouldn't hear the word NO

Don't be so caught up in the moment or yourself
That you can't step back and take a breath
When someone says that two-letter word NO
Just fall back and let it go

Voices Behind the Tears

"Too Young For Love"

Sixteen or Seventeen
Are they too young to be in love
Is it infatuation or hormones,
Or is it two trying to be grown?

On the phone day and night
She says, "I love you, Boo."
"Me too Baby." He replies
To him she vows to be true

As soon as he knows
He has her in his grasp
He flips the switch
And takes off his mask

He begins to control
Her every move
Has it cloaked in care
This cat is smooth

With her being so young
She thinks this is how love goes
Every move she makes
He always knows

Does he give the same to her
No, she's too scared to ask
The last time she dared to question
She found her throat in his grasp

Her friends are shocked and dismayed
"Girl, leave him alone!" is what they say
Yet, he's only acting out what he was shown
The lessons learned from childhood grown

They look and wonder why she stays

Saving Lives Through Lit

After all the signs he displays
Her story is the same as his
She grew up thinking this is the way it is

W. Kay Shabazz

Kay Shabazz specializes in marketing and public relations. A Westerville native, Kay earned a Bachelor of Arts degree in Marketing and Communications from The Ohio State University. She Manages Event Planning and Membership Support with Tech Columbus, where she focuses on membership retention, connecting businesses within the community and planning over 120 professional development and networking events during the year. A published author of the book HOLDING ON TO SOMEWHERE; Kay enjoys speaking to community audiences on the subject of family stability and domestic violence. Before joining Tech Columbus, Kay had a successful career as Marketing Director for The Martin Luther King Jr. Performing and Cultural Arts Complex.

WHY I WROTE:

Saving Lives Through Lit is an innovative approach to shed light on the many lives that are being torn apart and affected by domestic violence. I want my work to be a catalyst to helping eliminate domestic violence and the tolerance of it in our communities. I want to be part of the social change, in donating my time, talent & resources to support this program.

LINKS:
www.carbon2diamondpress.com
www.facebook.com/pages/Holding-ONTO-Somewhere

Excerpt from the novel: HOLDING ON TO SOMEWHERE

    The first time he hit me I was pregnant, in my fifth month, but barely showing. I wore baggy clothes and warm-up gear. I was in Texas for a visit celebrating my grant certificate from the city of Columbus to open a restaurant. Gbenga and I were happy and discussing the concept and interior of what the place would look like. I had already acquired a property that I could rent per month. It had formally been a strip club, but the grant money was really given to help improve the district with newer, more community-friendly businesses. Doors seemed to be opening, for Gbenga too. He had been working in communications at local television stations since he had left Texas Southern University. He always wanted to get into promotions and entertainment after working weekends, in which he spent with his cousin's band lining up shows and working as a soundman. Just one week prior, he was able to book one of the largest Reggae entertainers in the industry to perform at a show he was promoting at a local park. My heart was abloom with promise and excitement of the things to come for us. We just came back to his place after walking the dogs. He went upstairs to take a shower. All of a sudden his cell phone and his pager went off. I answered his cell phone. "Click!"

    I picked up the cell phone and the pager and carried both of them to the bathroom. The pager went off again.

    "69 911."

    Suddenly I became suspicious. Sixty-nine is a code synonymous for booty calls from the opposite sex. The phone rang again. I picked it up. "Hello."

    All I heard was quiet breathing and a woman's voice in the background. "Click!" I got to the bathroom, opened the door and put his phone and pager on the granite counter top.

    "Your phone was ringing and your pager is going off like crazy."

    "Who was it?"

    "I don't know? They hung up on me twice."

    The water from the shower stopped. I heard the shower door come open but I turned to walk down the steps. Ten minutes later Gbenga emerges from the bedroom wearing jeans and a Bob Marley t-shirt.

"I'll be right back. I need to buy some cigarettes," he said. Normally it wouldn't have struck me as anything, but I observed his posture as he was talking, very rushed and agitated.

Now the store is at the corner, a ten minute walk, but he left in the car. Twenty five minutes later, he spins into the driveway, cigarette resting in his mouth. He gets out of the car, comes in the house and starts rumbling in the cabinets.

"Baby, are you looking for something?" I said confused, judging by his demeanor. He didn't answer, but I could hear his pager vibrating in his pants pocket. "Gbenga, your pager is going off. Someone must really need to talk to you urgently," I said, with a tint of sarcasm in my voice. His face became overcast with clouds of darkness, and then all of a sudden, in one swift motion my mouth met with his backhand. I felt the soft flesh inside my bottom lip open, tasting blood and saliva.

"Did anyone ask you to pick up my phone? Why is your mouth so smart?" he said in a low dark voice, with lines on his forehead starting to appear.

I couldn't say a word, my eyes were watering, but I wasn't about to cry, I was stunned. I touched my lip as it was starting to swell. I looked up at him from the corner of my eye, lowered my eyelids and turned to walk away.

"I am sorry baby, I don't know what happened," he said apologetically, as though the slap from his backhand was a muscle spasm.

I packed my bags that day too, to leave and go home, but I stayed. That was the day I began to turn against myself, to question, not about leaving him, but about what I could have done to change what he did. I was partially at fault. Why did I get sassy? Even though he had told me to answer his phone several times before, maybe I shouldn't have picked it up. I was having his baby. If we were going to be a family, wouldn't that make him the head of the house? I started to feel bad that I was questioning him.

Chapter 4

STAPLES

Naming children at birth are the first pronouncements of love for your children. Sometimes they are given as predictions and affirmations. We named our sons after strong Black revolutionaries; Steven Biko, a South African who fought against Apartheid, and Malcolm X, "by any means necessary". Both were men of strength and purpose; they were leaders. Ironically, after the years of excuses and explanations to my children about what was happening when daddy was arguing with me behind the locked door, or how I had an accident, the fact that I gave them such strong names almost began to mock me. At night I would tuck them in with stories of brave men who stood up against numbers of people to do what they believed was right. I would kiss them on their foreheads and cower before a man who was oppressing my very existence. Every revolution has bloodshed and casualties. It wasn't fear of my blood being shed that gripped me night after night. Truthfully I was scared to change the channel on the television because it might set him off. It was the fear that my boys might become the casualties. I had long grown tired of Malcolm standing in as a referee during some of our arguments. He would be playing with his toys or watching cartoons when I noticed he would straighten up all of the sudden, drop his eyelids and cock his head. It was like a well trained dog that heard sounds that other people could not hear. Then Malcolm would spring up from wherever he was, go to the door and give his father a bear hug. It didn't happen all of the time, but after a while I noticed it happened whenever Gbenga's footsteps were slightly heavier against the marble floor, or if the sound the door made when it closed echoed louder against its wooden frame than usual. It was as though he was gauging his daddy's temperature by his movements and felt his hugs would become a coolant for his aggression. Sometimes he would be in his room when the fights started, and I would see a small shadow in the crack of the doorway. Then, I would walk into another room, aware I would be followed by my husband, but at least the fighting would not be in front of him. There were so many secrets we would hide. I became very good at making excuses and hiding bruises, which became a paradox. I would come up with excuses and stories to save him from embarrassment and ridicule. I became very convincing. But Gbenga was only convinced it made me a good liar, and as a liar I should be watched closely.

***

I pulled myself to his feet. Blood dripped on his toes as moved the trunk of my body upright. I rested my hand on his foot, massaging slowly in between his toes, as I did during much happier times, only this time it was blood and not baby oil. "Look at me, I'm here. I am right here. Put it down and hold me. We'll get through this." I moved up the side of his leg, only turning my head to rest on his knee, eyebrows stretching to keep my eyes peeled on the gun.

He sat, still bent over, stony-eyed, digging the gun deeper into his chest. "The hurting is going to stop tonight, I'll make it stop." I could feel his tears landing delicately on the top of my head. It wasn't only me he was fighting. He was fighting his own demons.

"We don't need to hurt each other. Let's try loving each other. What about the boys, baby?"

I spoke cautiously, holding his eyes with my gaze, and I saw something in his piercing eyes that few people ever had. It was a quiet desperation. He lowered the gun and set it on the bed. It took me a minute to shake myself out of my daze, letting all the words I wanted to say clutter the space in my head.

I had only remembered seeing Gbenga cry once. It was August of 1997, when he received the news that his icon, Fela, had died. It was an odd feeling, like seeing a lion carrying a baby antelope to safety between his enormous sharp teeth. When I pictured Gbenga, I never pictured him with his mouth foaming, pupils dilated, and standing over top of my broken body waving his fists. I had always pictured him with his hands wrapped gently around my waist, supporting me from behind while watching our boys play on the beach. I saw him grilling fresh fish in the back yard, as I looked out from the balcony of the beautiful mansion that we designed together in his village, as the boys splashed in the pool. He was the man who talked about building Black nations, and leaving legacies to his grandchildren. This to me was Gbenga, and that was who I wanted to grow old with. Even in the very worst times, I never saw myself as weak. I identified myself as humble. I never thought less of myself, I just thought about myself less. I saw the strength in unconditional love, an example of someone who would stick and stay. I understood that marriages take work, and no one would ever fill everything you desired. If they did, what would you need God for? Selfish people were the weak ones. They couldn't see past themselves. But to forgive shows humility. Forgiveness is tough; it takes a strong person to forgive. I wasn't interested and didn't see myself as a victim. I was a fighter, a conqueror, and love conquers all, right?

***

Most people don't fear the end of a relationship. It's not the sad part; it's the struggle of knowing how to begin again. The beginning, that's where the fear is. With Gbenga we were always starting over and I was always trying to get back to that place where we began, where I was confirmed and loved. I could think of him as a good bad man or a bad good man. Depending on which direction I wanted to hold onto. I should have taken more responsibility in my direction and a bit less caught up while being held. Being complacent and standing still was only meant to be long enough for me to catch my breath. It is not a destination. I know I have a unique blessing with my name on it, but I have to know who I am, not what other people say I am, or I will never recognize it.

I didn't see the detour. No one told me a wrong turn wasn't always identified with orange cones. I was dreaming, sinking, and soothing in a warm dark river of kisses. Kisses on necks and shoulders; every kiss a deliberate apology. The harder my shell, the deeper he would journey to reach me. Hmm… Gbenga, in this moment I feel safe being lost in you, distracted from pain, wet from love's juices and not from tears. The worrying about the boys, my own desires for a parent's love, all of it is lifted off of me and washed away by the ocean of tender kisses, maybe not for long but for now, and really, where else did I want to be?

Days rolled by as our relationship remained in a holding pattern. Or maybe I remained in a holding pattern as our relationship was rolling by.

Saving Lives Through Lit

***

I stuffed each of them between my breast and the wire along the cup of my bra. I took a few steps back to scan my room. I reflected on the hanging clothes, and those folded neatly on multiple cedar wood racks. The jewelry chest filled with 'bling' and baubles next to the espresso stained dresser, and the countless photo albums under the nightstand next to the bed. I wrote a letter:

When I thought about the love I had for you, I based it on count-less letters. Each one was filled with passion, submission, deep desires, obedience, forgiveness, sacrifice and unconditional love. The words taunted my heart and pierced my soul. It was perfect love with rewards that would outlast our grandchildren's grandchildren, passing through the end of time. Each letter was personal. I found the more I read, the deeper my understanding of the relationship grew. I stopped writing a long time ago. Every note you have given me you will find in a shoe box under the bed. The letters I refer to were from men I have never met, but they witnessed the love I strived to have. Even through the darkest moments in our relationship they encouraged me to hold on. Your insecurities and jealousies are confirmed, their names: Peter, Paul, Mark and John. I thought this relationship was my cross to bear; funny thing about a cross, it can lead to salvation, or it can be used for crucifixion. I just realized the difference, God has to be in it. He isn't in this. Good bye. Kim

Lavinia Thompson

My name is Lavinia Thompson. I am a 22-year old hippie who is just embarking upon my life's journey. I have emerged from the dark depths of domestic violence and abuse that ruled my childhood for so long. This road hasn`t been an easy one but I am discovering my voice. Writing has always been my escape and my outlet from the abuse. Even in the years after it ended, it was therapeutic for me. It is now my voice and I want it to be heard, to let other victims and survivors know that they are not alone and the cycle can be broken. There is hope, help and there is a day when the words "never again" really mean, never again. I want to be a part of making sure we all see that day.

WHY I WROTE:

It is important for me to participate in this anthology because the issue has impacted my life in every aspect. Almost a decade of abuse and witnessing what my own mother went through left deep scars. Writing was always my therapy but now I want it to be a voice and I want it to speak to people. I persevered over my own struggles during those years and in the destructive aftermaths. I am doing my own poetry book about child abuse, but I feel it is vital to be as active as possible in raising awareness about the issue in the best way possible, and for me that is in writing. I love the idea that proceeds go to a relevant charity. This is an ageless issue and it is one that needs to have awareness drawn to it or it'll never end. I am honored to be part of this. It means so much to me. I will be contributing poetry that is going to be included in my poetry book, She Wasn't Allowed to Giggle. It is a self-publishing project I am embarking on to be released this fall. Spellbound by Fire is my other project, to be released Sept. 15, 2011 through Hellfire Publishing. It is about a young witch who loses the aunt who raised her to witch hunters and has to find a way to survive on her own. Spellbound has a theme about breaking and preventing the cycles of violence and abuse.

LINKS:
My writer's blog:
www.laviniathompsonauthor.wordpress.com/
Facebook page for Spellbound:
 www.facebook.com/pages/Spellbound-by Fire/164218530279552
Facebook :
www.facebook.com/pages/Lavinia-Thompson/155049924551916
Twitter:
@LaviniaThompson

Blue Motel

I look
in a mirror.
She stares back at me.
Look back to the door;
she is there after all these years.
She is the child in me
wondering where to go from here,
washing dishes and staring
out to skies that should be
blossoming in spring.
All I see is winter.
This May I turn 21.
With a sigh of bitter discontent
it all looks the same after a while.

Duties of a mother
set to a ten year old.
She always made things proper.
Not a crumb on the plates.
Not a stain on the glasses.
Not a wrinkle in the beds
for fear of something out of place
was the reason he'd make her
scream at night.

Nostalgically she remembers
much more than I ever will.
In a letter to me she says
there's that blue motel where
Mother used to flee with us.
I'd be in the back seat with a bit of
grimace at the neon sign in the dark.
Mother would be lucky to have time
to pack overnight bags before ushering
us out the door into the car;
running.

Saving Lives Through Lit

Sometimes it seems you're
so far in somewhere
there is no getting out.
There are days it seems
I should be 30; like
childhood never existed.
It was there... I know it was
but like the moon in vanquishing phase
above motel rooftops
it was gone...leaving me here tonight
washing dishes, looking out the window.
There's a whisper in the winter storm
saying you can't go back,
don't ever look back.

Not a crumb on the plates.
Not a stain on the glasses.
Not a wrinkle in the laundry.
Life's like an hourglass of things
that can't be left for tomorrow.
It's a lot like yesterday.
I muse to random snowflakes clinging
to the kitchen window.
Where is my childhood?

From somewhere in the room
a little girl's voice whispers:
Behind you.

Voices Behind the Tears

Who Do You Think You Are?

When time ran out
the clattering pieces to this life fell apart;
all of the two faced masks people wear
turned away into death light of the sun
whenever you sat in that hotel bar room,
mother's blood on your hands.
How many times can you scream at night
beaten and tortured?
Truth a barbarous blow in a ruinous home…

Who do you think you are?

You'd stagger home from the bar
yelling and bellowing, bottle rendered broken
in your clenched hands, watched you throw
her around like a helpless rag doll…
everything is wrong.
When time ran out
blood was the shadowed war paint,
words slashing from the roof of your mouth
like a knife across the wrist tonight…
Someone's got hell to pay for the
nights of slamming doors, crashing pictures,
you always thought a sorry would
put them back together again…
Who do you think you are?

Acting now like nothing ever happened.
Go on and scream at me still
bruises over my face and no such tears.
Seems you can only scream so many times
before you're insensitive to
everything that's wrong.

When time ran out
the house was on fire, smoke

Saving Lives Through Lit

billowing black in the July skies,
torn apart, agonized, brutalized…
Swear I seen your shadow on that hill
watching, deathly wolf waiting for the kill.
On my knees screaming in the pouring rain;
truth one more resonating blow
on the desolate street.

Who do you think you are?

Two faced people still looked the other way
but how many times can you scream
before you just crumple to the sidewalk?
If I could stand strong with blood on my face
this would be the day they'd finally see you wrong,
this would be the day they'd be asking:

Who do you think you are?

But when time ran out
only nostalgic ashes remained.
A single butterfly flew round the remnants
of the house I grew up in,
Truth a delicate memory, precariously
bitter in its blood-drenched misery.
Around, around the flowers that butterfly
fluttered, I sat there alone in the summer dusk
orange dusted, knew nothing would ever
be the same…but the screams still echo…
I swear to this day…

Who do you think you are?

Down Her Face (War Paint)

War paint is red as blood down her face tonight.
War paint is white as stained lace as he leaves the room.
War paint is black as sadness in anger-streaked skies.
War paint is red as blood down her child's face tonight.
War paint is purple as skies that break with final truth.
War paint is a real color like colors are silent but
War paint is on the face of every woman.
War paint is red as the anger down her face tonight.

Kelli "Song Bird" Garden

I am a poetess/author, songwriter/vocalist. I started writing poe-try in the 7th grade as an outlet in understanding myself and the world around me, which was not always easy to verbally express. Over the years I've had my poetry included in anthologies and also, turned into songs. In July of 2010, I had my first poetry book pub-lished "Through The Storms (Poetry and Inspirational Writings)" by Kelli Garden.

It can be purchased at www.kelligarden.com, www.amazon.com and www.barnesandnoble.com. I've been a featured poet in Writer's Point of View Magazine and I'm in the process of being featured in two more. I've been a guest poet on Blogtalk Radio as well as Talkshoe Radio. I'm currently working on a CD, which will be a mix of songs written and spoken word with music. I have several other ventures that are in the workings as well. I can be found on Facebook as Kelli Garden and on Twitter as Songbirdg.

WHY I WROTE:

With my poetry, I hope to encourage, bring healing and hope to others. Being featured in the anthology is another opportunity to help others and also allow my voice to be heard and the gift of poetry to be kept alive.

LINKS:
http://www.vrtechmarketinggroup.com/KGarden2/
http://www.kelligarden.com

Come in Out Of the Rain

From all the heartache and pain;
It's time to come in out of the rain.
From the lies, abuse and people
mistreating you;
It's time to come in out of the rain.
From all the misunderstandings, the
verbal, mental and physical abuse;
It's time to come in out of the rain.
No longer will you allow the mis-
conceptions or disconnections of others
dictate your destiny. Nor will they
define or re-define who you are and
were designed to be.
They cannot destroy or touch the
essence of your inner strength and beauty.
It's time, Yes! It's time to come in
out of the rain.
No more tears of heartache and pain.
Your tears are now tears of joy.
Your dance is of victory.
It's your time, your season beloved,
to come in out of the rain.

Kelli Garden

Leave the Mess

When they deny what you know to be
a lie, and the things they do hurt
and make you cry.
Wipe the tears from your eyes.
Hold your head high.
Look to the sky.
Look unto the One who holds the key.
He alone will supply every one of
your needs.
With the love of the Father,
He will bring you through it and to it;
To a better and brighter day.
With the truth, faith, and the
resurrected power of Christ on the
inside of you; walk away with
confidence and pride.
Into your deliverance;
for God is on your side.
The power of God's love surrounds
and encompasses you.
Leave the mess.
Seek God's best.
Never settle for less.
Realize you are too truly blessed!

--Kelli Garden

He Loves Me, He Loves Me Not
(Poem for Lawanda)

He was fine as wine and he noticed me, talked to me and wanted me to be his girl. Isn't that something?
He said he loved me and oh did I love him! My high school sweetheart… Stan the man!
I remember the first time he hit me and beat me on the street. He said he was sorry and that he loved me.
With each child we had together his love still remained. He'd hit and beat me every chance he got… his love for me never changed.
We've been married and together close to thirty years. I remember my children shielding my body with their little bodies, protecting me from their daddy's love. He loves me… It was my pitiful refrain.
Don't ask me why I made so many excuses or why I stayed and didn't get away. Because he loves me… is all I have to say.
I knew it was coming eventually. His promise he would keep. His brand of love was intense and deep, my pleas, words, and my screams this time would all go unheard.
He dragged me into the tub, with a shotgun in his hand. For hours he punched, beat, and stomped me over and over and over again.
With such an evil, hateful rage in his eyes, I knew this time I would surely die. I could hear neighbor's plea for him to stop. As my heart was bursting within my chest, my body bleeding and racked in pain; I thought about many things such as my children and how I loved them so. Why did I never have the courage to get up and go? I thought about the Bible and God's word that said, "Love is patient and kind. Love doesn't hurt or harm." As the brain matter oozes out of my head and splatters into the bathtub, I take my last breath. These are the words that ran through my hurting head: He loves me, He loves me not. As my spirit departs my battered and beaten body, He loves me. He loves me not. I now realize, he never did.

Chamani J Carter

Chamani J Carter is a young bright young girl who has a big heart. She enjoys singing, taking pictures, cooking and playing with her younger siblings. She is the middle child with 3 older siblings and 2 younger, between both her father and her mother. She resides currently in Virginia with her mother, step-father and younger brother.

Although Chamani has witnessed lots of arguing and some fight-ing between adults growing up, her worst nightmare happened when she was 8 years old, on Mother's Day. It was a day that changed her life forever.

With big dreams of being a model, actress, singer, cook and author, Chamani is on her way to fulfilling her big dreams. She fully intends to let nothing stop her from seeing her name in lights one day.

WHY I WROTE:

I wrote to this book, because I wanted other young kids that have gone through what I have to know that they are not alone. I want them to know it's okay to tell and not to be scared. I hope to write a book and be able to fully share my story and give hope and strength to others.

LINKS:
ChamaniJCarter.webs.com
Diamondstar_Entertainment@yahoo.com

MY WORST DAY EVER

Your parents always tell you that if anyone hurts you to come to them, they will protect you. They tell you that no one has the right to do anything to you that you don't want them to do. They assure you that no matter if it is an adult, a child, your father, uncle, or friend of the family, no means no, and you have a right to say no and be heard. But, when you're a child, you innocently never think anything bad can ever happen to you. You never think anyone you know would ever hurt you. Unfortunately, you trust everyone, especially those that you know and care for. You never imagine that anyone you laugh with, hug, talk to, eat with, and claims to love you, could ever do anything to hurt you.

But, on May 11th, 2008 my innocent world came to an immediate and earth shattering halt. On Mother's Day, of all days, I learned just how true my mother's words were when she said she'd be there for me. I also learned the terrible truth that everyone isn't trustworthy.

It was just a regular normal holiday. My younger brother, my upstairs neighbors, and the kids from next door and I, were outside just having fun. We were doing what kids do; running around, screaming, laughing, getting fussed at by our parents for running in and out the house, you know everyday stuff. Little did I know that my innocence was moments away from being stolen. Had I known, I would have stayed in the house for sure and avoided all that was about to take place.

The day quickly went from upbeat and fun to scary and traumatic. My brother went home to eat lunch and my upstairs neighbors went home, as well, but I stayed to play with the boy from next door. He and I have played many, many times before. His sister was my God-mother, so I felt safe. It wasn't even a second thought, even when his older brother came over too and wanted to play hide and seek with us. I thought cool. Maybe I should have known better. Maybe I should have left when the other girls I was with went home. Maybe I should have never stayed to play with two boys. But I guess when you're young, you're also naïve. I thought we were all friends, practically family.

Hi, my name is Chamani Carter and I'm a rape victim. Talk about scary. Talk about wanting to die. Talk about wanting to run and hide. I was there and so much more. He was 15 years old, I was 8, and I didn't know what to do. After his brother left and I was getting ready to leave he took me by the hand and pushed me down to the ground on my stomach. I was afraid and confused. But when he pulled down my pants and tried to put his thing in me, I screamed. He told me if I wasn't quiet and if I told anyone, the police would come and they would take me away from my mom. He spit on me back there, and I was disgusted. Why was he spitting on me? Nasty! But then I figured out why. Talk about pain, it was unbearable. I couldn't believe it. Why was he doing this to me? He was my older brother's friend. He had been to my house playing with his X-Box, or basketball in the yard. Why me? What was I going to do when he was done? Was he going to hurt me, hit me, or kill me? Then just as fast as it began it was over. He let me up and reminded me of what would happen if I told anyone. Then he walked away like it was nothing.

All I could do was run home. I was covered in dirt and scared my mother was going to yell at me. So when she came to the door, I apologized for being dirty and told her I fell playing next door. Luckily I was so upset and in tears, she smiled and just told me to go and take a shower. You know those movies where the woman scrubs and scrubs, well that was me. I was crying, and trying to be as quiet as I could, so that my mom didn't hear me and ask any questions. But I hurt so bad, and was so ashamed.

After my shower I went to into the hallway with my two best friends from upstairs. I guess they could see I was upset and asked what was wrong. I told them what the boy next door did to me and I cried. The older of the two girls, picked me up and held me. They wanted me to tell my mom. But I was scared of what he said would happen if I told. I begged them not to say anything. They kept assuring me nothing bad would happen. I guess my mom heard us fussing or me crying or something and came out to see what was up. They told her I was hurt. I just stared at her, I couldn't say anything. I wanted someone else to say it. Maybe then nothing bad would happen. I wouldn't be the one who told. But, no one said a word. My mom was getting irritated because I was upset and wouldn't tell her what was wrong. I was crying and with my two good friends holding my hands, I confessed what had just happened.

My first thought was, okay, we are going to have to leave and they are going to come and take me away. At the same time I wanted to move not away from my mom, but away from the boy who had hurt me. I would have to leave my friends though and it was unfair. My mom picked me up in her arms and held me. I cried, and I apologized. She told me it wasn't my fault. She took me right next door to face him. He denied it, but my mom was strong. She pointed out to his family the dirt all over him that was all over me. She told them she still had my clothes and that they had his DNA on them. Then she called 911. It was so scary. I thought for sure they were going to come and lock me up. But they didn't.

They took me and my mom to Baystate Hospital so I could get checked out. I had to tell the story over and over again. The doctor had to look at me where he hurt me. My mom brought my clothes and gave them to the police man. It seemed to take forever. I felt so bad, because my mom was so upset and all alone there with me. She told me not to worry, that I was her princess and she didn't blame me, reassuring me that it wasn't my fault. She kept saying that. Every time she said it I'd cry, because I felt I should have known better. I was embarrassed I let it happen to me. Why didn't I fight him?

Eventually my mom told my father. I think she was really scared to tell him. She didn't want him to blame her and say she wasn't watching me correctly and she didn't want him to do anything to get himself in trouble. I heard her sometimes talking to him, telling him to calm down and not do anything to get himself locked up. I'm glad he listened. I would have felt really, really guilty if my dad had done something because of what happened to me.

Though the boy went to jail for kids his age for a little while, he got out. They made him live somewhere else until my mom found us a new place to live that wasn't next door to his family. That was the hardest 6 months. It was hard to live there. It was hard to go to school. I think my friends that were there for me the day it happened turned on me and told everyone at school. When I went to school, my younger sister knew and other kids knew. I was crushed. Again someone who I trusted had betrayed me.

Eventually my mom found me a therapist. All I was doing was crying. It was nice and scary talking to someone about how I felt. But she also helped me to figure out what I could do to feel better. My therapist name was Jackie. I will always remember her. She was very nice to me. She helped me relax and understand that it really wasn't my fault; that he had the issue and not me. I was able to forgive myself and not blame myself anymore. It's still hard sometimes. Sometimes when I hear the boy's name my stomach still feels weird, even if it's not him someone is talking about.

Though the boy that hurt me, didn't get charged or really have to pay for what he did to me, they said he didn't understand what it was he did was wrong. But, I still have to live with the pain and the shame for the rest of my life. I think that is unfair. He got away with hurting me, and people probably think I lied. But you know what? I learned how much those words really mean. When my parents told me they would be there for me forever; they couldn't prevent me getting hurt, but once they knew I was hurt, my mom sprang into action and protected me. And my dad was right by her side! They circled me and did what they had to do to try to make me better and never stopped telling me that they loved me.

I know it's hard to tell. I know it's scary, you don't know what will happen. But I'm glad I told.

God knows what happened to me, and I can only imagine that He put the strength that I needed in me. I don't know how else I and my family faced this. For a while it tore us apart. But we were all able to face this horrible thing. I learned how strong I am. All because I didn't listen to my abuser and I listened to my inner voice and I told.

I didn't let me attacker win.

Instead, I won!

Tamyara Brown

My name is Tamyara Brown. I was born and raised in Brooklyn, NY. I now reside in Buffalo, NY. I am a single mother of six beautiful children and two grandchildren. I am a writer and my first novel Fat Girl Vigilante will be released winter 2011. I have loved writing since I was eleven years old. I also have worked in Customer Service for a number of years.

The first time I saw abuse was when I was six years old. I saw my stepfather striking my mother with a belt as if she was child. She lay there helpless, as a victim to the man she loved. I'll never forget her words, "I'll change and do whatever you want me to do. Just stop hitting me." I too became a victim of Domestic Violence and muttered those exact words years later. So this is an honor to contribute my skills and energy to this anthology.

WHY I WROTE:

Following the same pattern of being in an abusive relationship, I hope to use my writing as a tool to inspire someone that they shouldn't be treated less than a woman. To help them know that love isn't being beaten nor mistreated. That life goes on after an abusive relationship and you too can survive. I use my writing to heal not only my soul but hope it will help someone break free from being the victim and become victorious.

LINKS:
tam4loyd@gmail.com
Web Pages: www.tamluvstowrite.weebly.com
Twitter: tamluvstowrite @twitter.com
Facebook: facebook.com/tamyarab

My apology to Amy

Sitting in this jail cell has made me think a lot about the day I shot my beloved Amy. I made the mistake of pulling the trigger and almost taking her life. My mentality was if I couldn't have her no one could and I'll admit I was a selfish man. Amy loved me unconditionally, even after her family denounced me and two ex-girlfriends testified that I was a beast.

She stayed with me. It was their fault, at least I thought, in the beginning for brainwashing her against me. When the truth began to seep in her like venom, she was unable to love me enough to stop the hitting. I went over the edge and did the unthinkable.

I've sat here for a number of years and there's not a second I don't regret what I have done to my sweet Amy.

If I could turn back the hands of time I would have let her go. Pride and selfishness caused me to choose the wrong path. Amy, my sweet Amy I was supposed to bring you roses for no reason and not because I blackened your eyes. My kisses shouldn't have been to heal the pain that I caused. The nights I screamed at you should have really been sweet tender words of kindness. Now that I think about it, you believed in me more than I did myself. You loved me more than I loved myself, unconditionally.

I showed love by calling you bitch instead of beautiful. The nights you only wanted to please me I chose to mistreat you. What was going on in my head to have poured out so much hate against a woman who loved me so deep? I sit in my cell and cry tears of agony and hurt.

Realizing the hands of times will not turn back because the hands of time don't stop for any woman or man. I marinate in guilt and shame. I marinate in self-pity of doing the crime of possibly taking away her spirit to love another man. I soak in tears that she will forever hate me and not have the heart to forgive; at least I assume.

I took the route my father did with my mother and so many countless women he used as a punching bag. I inherited his hate for women. I'm not blaming my father for my actions as a man who has years on his sentence and Amy's blood on my hand. I take full responsibility for the abuse I inflicted on her and any woman who crossed my evil path.

Some of the tears that flood this cell are the same ones I cried over my mother, who endured years of abuse by my father. I should have known better. Maybe, just maybe, my anger steamed from when she put me in jail for trying to save her life and protect her from his punches. It lingered in my head that she wanted to be beat after having the cop's place the cuffs on my wrist instead of my father's, who brought bodily harm to her body. I took that out on every woman afterwards. I never talked about it.

My father advised me during the first time he beat me with an extension cord, "Real men don't cry." I wish back then that I had shared my pain and disgruntled feelings. Then, maybe Amy would have been free of the pain I inflicted on her. I wish I had cried on Amy's shoulder instead of shooting her in the back and taking away her ability to walk.

I have always used my voice to express anger and deceit. Today I would like to use my voice to express my deepest apology to Amy for hurting her the way I have. I ask God to forgive me for the man I became and have mercy on my soul. When I am free in seventeen more years I will never hit another woman. While I am in here I'm getting the help I need. I know that it is hard to believe but this my open letter to Amy, letting her know that I apologize for abusing her and taking her love for granted.

Are You Ready to See?
By Tamyara Brown

I'm blind to the fact that hitting me isn't love.
The imprint of the word "Bitch" has now become my name.
As you branded me as being less than human…
Every time I try to leave you inform me
No one will ever love me
And fear has overcome me.
I chose you for all the wrong reasons
I don't ever want to be lonely
I thought being mistreated was the name of the game
Never knew I deserved to be treated kind
Never knew that hugs and kisses were free.
His love cost the price of me losing the existence of me
The mirror reflection of an eye painted black.
In the dark truth came to light
Opened my eyes to see
Love never should cost a thing
His handprint should not be my mark of beauty
My blindfolds are off and I clearly see.
The beauty that I have inside of me
The strength to let go and leave.
The question had been asked, "Are you ready to see?"
Yes I said, as I close the door on that chapter of my life,0
Yes, Yes I am ready to see?

Terrell Mercer

Terrell K. Mercer would tell you there is nothing much to him other than he is just here. A closer look would let you know otherwise. He has been given many titles by others yet they all pale in comparison to servant. Serving God in serving his fellow man is his driving force and passion. He shares his highs as well as his lows in life just to help his fellow man overcome. If he knows it can be a help or blessing to another he will pour it out to be read or heard.

"Life, Hymns & Love Notes, "published by Revolutionary Dis-ciples, is his first published work but don't let the title think it's just for the "churched." Applying the principle of, "being in the world but not of the world," Terrell poetically addresses various issues concerning both the physical & spiritual being of his fellow man. Along with his CD, "The Audible Experience," Terrell is seeking to stimulate & educate the mind of his fellow man. With his message of, "Don't just speak on life but speak TO life," he comes with a message to challenge his fellow man to aspire to greater things in life

WHY I WROTE:

As a male I feel not just my voice but the voice of many males need to be heard & expressed in this matter that has gripped our society for far too long. We have been silent too long on a "plague" in which we, men, are a majority perpetrator & minority victim. It is a must I do my part to help end this vicious cycle of abuse any way, shape or form that I can. I have been blessed with a gift to inspire through words & I will push it to its fullest potential to reach whom it needs to reach.

LINKS:
Twitter: @terrellkmercer
Facebook: Terrell K. Mercer
http://www.myhelpmyhope.org/
http://www.reverbnation.com/terrellk

1 Corinthians 13:4-7 (NIV) Love is patient, love is kind. It does not envy, it does not boast, it is not proud. It is not rude, it is not self-seeking, it is not easily angered, it keeps no record of wrongs. Love does not delight in evil but rejoices with the truth. It always protects, always trusts, always hopes, always perseveres.

8: Love never fails……..
"At times we don't appreciate love because we don't know how to receive it."
Bishop Lewis L. Stokes Sr.

LOVE I'M SORRY

See love, you never failed me but I've failed you
They say that you're an action word
Yet, I've not acted on all you truly are
I've been self-centered and self-absorbed
Throwing you out like a yo-yo
Out far and long enough
So when you come- you return
With something for me
And then, I throw you out again
You, as a word alone
You're so appealing
I've abused your true purpose
To explain how I'm feeling
Love I'm sorry
I've had my own selfish use of you
To build walls for others to climb
I've used you to reason my anger
And other thoughts in my mind
I've not shown the same patience
Nor kindness
That you've shown for me
So please forgive me
Love I'm Sorry

Voices Behind the Tears

How Can I Say…

How Can I say I love you?
How Can I say I care?
How Can I say I love you?
When the way I treat you is unfair.
How can I say I love you when almost every word that spews out of my mouth over you is set up to degrade?
And I seem to find fault in almost every meal in which you lovingly prepared & made.
"I mean your cooking's aight but I only eat it cause I'm hungry,'
"It's not like you cook good like my grandma, my mama or my aunty"
How can I say I love you when instead of speaking on the beauty of you I'm too busy focusing on what you're not?
Knowing you giving me 100% of you and I'm looking like, "Really is that the best you got?"
And what kind of love is this if I'm constantly talking about your weight
You gave birth to my children & I've got the nerve to talk about your stretch marks and call you out of shape.
"I mean can't you do some PX-90, some Zumba or something?
I spend time comparing you to other women I'm lusting & want-ing
"Why you can't be more like her or her," I'd constantly say
Until you get fed up & try to defend yourself one day
"OH I KNOW YOU'RE NOT TRYING TO TALK BACK"
I stand up look you dead in the eye & reach my hand back to _____
How Can I say I love you?
How Can I say I care?
How Can I say I love you?
When the way I treat you is unfair…
Your face stays caked up in make-up to cover up the blacks & blues,
Your vision stays blurry the blows causing you to see things in two's,
"I only do it because I love you," that statements so perverted
And I've somehow got you thinking that you actually deserve it
That's sad you've gotten so used to the verbal abuse & physical assault
That you even tell your friends that it's all your fault

And after every time I promise I won't do it again
Just never question where I'm going or ask where I've been
And after one time too many of knocking you to the floor
I hear you lowly mumble you can't take this any more
I yell "WHAT YOU GONNA DO," as you get up and run
I chase you into the room & you pull out a _____
How Can I say I love you?
How Can I say I care?
How Can I say I love you?
When the way I treat you is unfair
The moral of this story, so many have been believing
& living the lie that love is blind
Apostle Paul once wrote that love is patient & love is kind
Love may suffer long but it doesn't boast that mean it doesn't brag
But not once have I read or heard that love makes you a punching bag
How can I even have the right to say I'm a man?
If instead of showing you the firmness of my heart I show the firmness of my hand
I need to speak into your life & remind you of your worth
YES sticks & stones break bones but ladies & gentleman words DO hurt
If I say that this is love I should do so in truth how I'm supposed to
Cause if it's anything contrary how can I say that I love you?

Voices Behind the Tears

I Suffer……..

I suffer in silence because I know if I said anything I would be
thought of as being lesser than
If many knew the things that I suffer thru they'd question my claim to
the title of A MAN
How can I say it proudly & loudly knowing what happens behind
closed doors?
How could I show my face amongst family, friends & in public stores
Besides no one would believe me because many think
your femininity makes you weak
They never notice how I look at you first
almost for approval before I speak
I can feel your eyes cut me as each syllable begins to flow
Waiting for you to mouth the words,
"JUST WAIT UNTIL WE GET HOME!"
I suffer in silence because I was raised that a man
never strikes the one he loves
So I hold to this amongst the slaps, punches & shoves
I bite my lip, one tear flows you yell I'm crying like a punk
You slam the door, I sit on the floor & my head begins to slump
In the beginning I didn't think anything of it
as you degraded me with words
Yes sometimes they hurt but I never responded
to your venomous slurs
I felt that if I just loved you whatever
was causing this would soon erase
Until one day, not sure what I said, you slapped me in the face
To me it echoed and time stood still
My initial reaction was to punch you dead in the grill
You even looked at me like it was what you wanted
Pointed your finger in my chest, "I dare you do it,"
is what you taunted
Now still we stand, well not steadily but I'm right beside you
Though in your eyes I know you see me as beneath or behind you
I suffer in silence all in the name of love or least
I say that's what he have
Even though every time I say I do - you walk away & laugh

Saving Lives Through Lit

One day, just maybe I will stand to you in defiance
One day I will encourage others like me to no longer suffer in silence

Tony "The Logical" Wade

Born in Springfield, Massachusetts, Tony is the eldest of six, father of two, who currently resides in Virginia with his fiancée, their son, and his step daughter. Tony leans towards his spiritual background and faith for direction when making decisions. Between his love for music, which was planted deep in him as a youth, and his desire to help others, he took and nourished his skills turning his love of music into a business. He created DiamondStar Entertainment to help youth who have a desire to sing and make music. He began by lending his assistance to the church's music ministry. Later this led to giving vocal lessons and managing artist and groups. Tony's goal was to take those with a strong desire and steady focus and assist them in exploring how far their talent could take them.
Alongside Kiexiza Rodriquez, Tony is the co-host of the TonynKieShow, a weekly BlogTalkRadio held on Monday's at 6 p.m. EST. TNK listeners have dubbed the couple the "Baddest Fiancé Duo on Radio", for their neighbors next door, chilling with friend's, as a method of conversation and interviewing.

Tony is an aspiring author, working on his debut novel "Vengeance Unleashed," which is scheduled to be released December of 2011. He has several books planned to be released, including a poetry book and collaboration with another author.

WHY I WROTE:

Growing up the oldest of my siblings, I've seen abuse and have been victimized as well. It is never good to be hit or to hit, even in self-defense. But, it seems if you're a man and defend yourself, you are still viewed by society, as the abuser.

Seeing family and friends abused, led me to develop a soft spot in my heart for anyone man, woman or child who endures any kind of abuse. Often times it's the people on the outside who feel as helpless as the ones enduring the abuse. We may not be going through the physical pain, but we want to help and can't figure out how to get the ones we love out of the situation.

I pray this project goes very far in its attempt to reach out to and help victims and the agencies that give them strength to walk away.

LINKS:
Twitter: www.twitter.com/teestone419
Facebook: www.facebook.com/authortonywade
Website: www.authortonywade.webs.com
Blog: www.authortonywade.wordpress.com
Business website: www.Diamondstarentertainment.webs.com
Radio Show: www.blogtalkradio.com/TonynKieShow

THE ABUSE IS DONE

I always believed in a glimmer of hope;
that shining light up ahead;
Amazing considering the painful memories that
Built up over time in my head...
Now to those who knew my plight
and did nothing to help,
Who didn't believe me, and showed
me little concern...
You left me at a point when I needed you most,
And was at that point of no return...
Don't worry about me,
As far as what kind of friend or family member
You are... lesson learned!
You see, I have survived;
And the day of judgment for the one who tried
To steal my life and soul has arrived.
So I don't need you any more...
Yet I do thank you for those times when I needed
You, but you left me alone;
It taught me that I finally had to defend myself, stand up for my-self,
And be strong on my own!
He made his disdain for me so plain to see,
But you turned a blind eye;
Often he'd beat the hell out of me, and it wasn't an
Option in my mind for me to flee,
And although you'd see me in the window crying,
you'd simply walk by...
Why?
Was it none of your concern?
Did you feel nothing when you saw me in the store?
With bruises on the side of my face, and the back of my
hands covered with cigarette burns?
I know, I know...
You said to yourself, "I'm just the neighbor";
Heard my screams and figured because I was pregnant
It may be the pain from me going into labor...

Saving Lives Through Lit

By the way, that baby I lost…
You didn't know?
I miscarried when he beat it out of me
as he called me a whore…
Still can feel the pain from when he slammed
me into our bedroom door…
Not enough strength to leave on my own;
I remember how I loved him so…
If I left, I had no money, no job, and no place where I could go.
He was all I ever did know…
I often wondered, "Where did his love for me go?"
I guess I'll never know…
The blood coming from his chest doesn't flow slowly.
I should feel sad, maybe hurt from all I've lost,
But all I feel is FREE from his abuse…
His kicks and his vicious hits!
No more sore necks from where he
placed his oversized Mitts!
No more being slammed up against the wall!
No more being grabbed by my hair,
and dragged down the hall!
No longer will I shake uncontrollably as I face
the barrel of his gun,
as he waves it at me, grinning, like he's having fun!
I reached my breaking point and took all I could take
when he threatened my baby girl!
I had no choice but to act, for my child's sake!
I got a hold of his gun…
When, at me and my daughter he started to run…
I pointed it at him as he smiled at me daringly…
Never felt my hand squeeze the trigger
As he fell at my feet… you all want to gather
from the sound of my freedom's blast
go back into your homes, don't worry now…
the abuse… done.

Voices Behind the Tears

<u>Stop The Violence!</u>

Everything was rosy, till the day
Sara started getting hurt.
It started with words, they went from
Not so bad to worse.
Insults would hit her ears like hot
Water to skin,
Who said names could never hurt you?
They lied!
No matter what she did for him, she
Just couldn't win.
Then came the threats…
In her mind Sara thought to herself,
"He loves me. He said he did, so it
Must be true",
Yet every Friday night when he got
Home from the bar, it was her arms
That ended up sore, black and blue.
It lasted for months, and months turned
To years;
He paid all the bills and she had no where
To go…
He knew all that, plus she loved him,
so he played on her fears.
One day he came home and the dinner
Wasn't done;
Enraged, he started throwing things at her,
But she loved him, so for her it wasn't an
Option to run.
When her friends found out she refused to
to leave after all that he had done, they asked
poor Sara most abrasively,
"What's the matter with you?! Do you think
he's doing this crap for fun?"
But Sara wouldn't give up on her man, that's
not what she was taught;
her mother always said "You stick by your man

like I did with your father,
even though we always fought."
The abuse continued as a few more years passed.
Her friends pleaded with her, "Please leave this
beast! You don't know what he'll do!"
Sara got angry and kicked them all out, and said,
"Don't say another word! This conversation we're
having is through!"
That same night he got mad,
pushed her into the frig, and punched her
straight up in her jaw.
When he left the police came and said, "You want to
file a restraining order? The next time he tries anything,
you'll be fully protected by the law."
She thought, 'If I do this he'll hate me and beat me again. Then
where will my daughter and I live?'
So she sent them away,
figured she'd make this thing work,
and give it all she had to give.
After all, it was her fault she thought.
His dinner wasn't done,
she deserved that punch;
and being thrown into the wall.
She should've packed what he LIKED for lunch.
It was her fault.
The next night he came home, madder than the night before.
"You called the cops on me?! Who do you think you are?!
You're not leaving me! You're not walking out that door!"
Across the floor she flew, and into the wall with a 'THUD',
and she bled from her head as he took a sip of his BUD.
Terror swept over her, she was weak
and had nowhere to run,
she looked up in time to see him walk over to her bloodied
body, revealing his gun.
"You had to make me mad! Look what you've done!
You had to go and piss me off! Hope it was worth it! Did you
have fun?!"
"JEFFREY..., PLEASE, NO!"

Voices Behind the Tears

"Stop your whining Sara! You wanted our marriage to end,
so fine! Here we go!"
And with that he pulled the trigger, and Sara was shot in the head;
the next day her best friend found her on the floor, and her
5 year old daughter lay shot in the bed.
Many who were hurt cried at their funeral that week,
but no one knew what was left to be said;
Sara waited and hoped that this mad man would change,
and as a result,
her and her daughter ended up dead.

IT'S DOMESTIC VIOLENCE AWARENESS MONTH
PLEASE PEOPLE... STOP THE VIOLENCE!

~TONY WADE~

Envy Red

Envy Red is a Washington, DC area native by way of Birmingham, Alabama. A two time graduate of the University of Maryland, she resides in Southern Maryland with her two boys. A passion spawned long before she was diagnosed with and survived a rare form of cancer. She is driven by a firm desire to make a charitable mark on society. As the founder of the "Free Minds Project," a youth and prison outreach program, Envy Red is dedicated to promoting literacy, helping individuals realize their potential, and achieving their dreams. As a board member of Homebound Citizens Non Profit, assisting homebound citizens and the homeless population, the journey to help others shall be realized one person at a time.

WHY I WROTE:

I would like to be a part of the "Saving Lives Through Lit" project because it creates awareness of a social issue that I have first-hand knowledge. As a child I bore witness to the effects of domestic violence on shaping a young mind into a troubled adult psyche. At a young age I went from witness to victim. Fortunately, I was able to quickly recover from that experience. Everyone is not blessed with that opportunity but this campaign can help change that. I would like to bring awareness to this troubling subject and assist others in overcoming and breaking this vicious cycle of abuse before it is too late. I am committed to helping individuals plant their feet on a path of new and promising beginnings. A path of greatness where the sky has no limits!

LINKS:
Social Networks:
www.facebook.com/EnvyRed
www.twitter.com/EnvyRed
www.authorsinfo.com/envyred
Official Website:
www.envyred.com/

Sweetest Hangover

By: Envy Red

"Well, if I haven't learned anything this semester, I have learned to fix the exterior," I spoke softly to my own reflection in the oval shaped bathroom mirror.

I gave an exaggerated chuckle at the tear stained image in the mirror but only momentarily, as I flinched from the fresh wave of pain the peroxide caused as I tried again, as I had in the past, to fix my latest infliction.

These days, my training in med school came in handy more in my personal life than passing any exam the professors at Georgetown could challenge me with.

"Bitch!... Uhhh, I mean Karrine, honey, please open the door," Jay said, banging on the bathroom door which was both locked and barricaded.

Great emphasis was placed on the word "bitch" and far less on the meager attempt to clean it up. I had become accustomed to that word over the past year of our fifteen month relationship. I barely remembered the honeymoon phase of the first ninety days, which was now a distant memory replaced with the brutal realities of right now.

My heart jumped and skipped a beat, as the love of my life gave the door what sounded like a final kick, before storming down the hallway and leaving remnants of a large grunt and the mumbling of something inaudible in the air outside my tiny bath room door. Most likely it was an obscenity about what was in store for me in the future for my blatant defiance.

I exhaled slow and deep as I dabbed at my left eye which had taken the form of a large golf ball and quickly filled with blood stealing any sign of the beauty others raved about and I humbly accepted to appease their persistence.

Truth is I hated the attention that their blue grey tone commanded against my caramel complexion. They were compliments of my father who many would simply describe as a mixed breed. Besides the somber gray eyes, I had also inherited his height standing at a staggering 5'10", which was considered more than tall for a female. As a result, I spent most of my life feeling awkward and "growing into" myself.

BAM!

The sound of the front door slamming caused my body to flinch and a fresh wave of silent tears to run down my cheeks in a steady stream.

At the still tender age of twenty five, I was in my second year of med school at the nationally acclaimed Georgetown University School of Medicine. I remember being as proud as one could be when I began my first semester that bright and sunny day in late August of 2010.

The process to get in was grueling to say the least. There were over 11,500 applicants of which only approximately 1,100 were chosen for interviews. The end result was a mere 420 students being accepted into the program.

Words couldn't describe the feeling of euphoria that swept over me when I received the letter welcoming me as one of the chosen few. It surpassed the proud feeling that overcame me as my parents watched me walk across the stage of the University of Maryland to receive my B.S in Biology less than one year prior. I graduated with a solid 3.8 GPA and an immediate job offer at a research lab in Washington, DC.

Upon receiving my acceptance letter to med school in the late winter month of March 2010, I remember being too excited to wait to call my parents who were away from their Ashburn, VA mansion on business to the Cayman Islands. Both were engineers for a large corporation that chartered various small jets to the elite and often famous clientele.

"Oh my goodness... Michael come here!", my mother exclaimed as I heard her fumble with her blackberry.

I could hear the concern in my father's voice as he questioned what had my mother Lauren so excited.

I could almost see the worry lines spreading across his pale complexion and him running his fingers through his salt and pepper colored beard. This was a nervous habit he had for as long as I could remember.

"We are on speaker Karrine, please bring magic to my ears one more time honey," my mother said, in her sweet and nurturing tone trying her best to sound calm.

Standing tall despite her petite 5'1" slim frame, with a brown sugar complexion, full lips, and high cheek bones, she had beautiful prominent features. Her dark slanted eyes were compliments of her mother's Asian roots. She kept her gray streaked main cropped short and stylish. Both of my parents were in their mid 50's and were what most would consider a power couple having great success in their personal lives as well as their career.

"I got into Georgetown's School of Medicine!" I practically screamed again into the receiver as I jumped up and down in place from excitement.

"That's my baby girl!" My father's voice boomed with pride.

"We'll be home in two days ladybug," my mother said.

"We must celebrate at your favorite restaurant," she continued with excitement still illuminating from her voice.

I could picture her beautiful smile as she sank into my father's embrace. His tall lean frame was most likely planted firm behind her, nerves now replaced with papa bear pride.

"Sounds great guys I love you both, kisses see you soon!" I exclaimed, before hitting the end button but not a second before catching bits and pieces of my father's "that's my baby girl" in the background.

Ironically, it would be a celebration that would never take place and in fact mark the beginning of the end of all celebrations for me. Exactly two days later, on the day they were to return, both died in a tragic plane crash over the waters of the Atlantic just outside of Florida. No one aboard the small chartered vessel survived, including my parents, their business partner, his wife, and the pilot. There would be no celebration or even goodbyes for that matter. Instead, I got to replay the devastation over and over on the evening news in the days to come.

I was their only child, the sole surviving heir to their short lived legacy. In the months to come I would learn news that I was com-pletely unprepared for. Although they appeared to live a fabulous life, they were swimming in debt. The rather large trust fund they set aside for my continued education and head start in life had been depleted a few years earlier and not without penalty. They had seemingly been able to fund my undergraduate year's debt free. Unlike my peers, I was not overcome with student loan repayments upon exiting college. However, I soon learned the harsh reality was that my parents had covered it instead with an unimaginable debt of their own.

Upon their death, my dreams of med school appeared to fade as quickly as they had from my life. Nevertheless, against my closest friend's Shelly's advice, I took out a loan and started med school that August with my parent's death still fresh. Almost immediately the student loan figures mounted and surpassed anything I had ever become accustomed to seeing next to my name.

Furthermore, the job at the lab was not doing much to cover the living expenses for my small one bedroom apartment near campus or the vehicle I was forced to purchase with the little credit I did manage to obtain. Unfortunately, my C class Mercedes had been taken away along with all of my parent's other assets upon settlement of their estate. It was one that ended with large zeroes for me as the beneficiary when the dust settled and cleared.

Having migrated to the DC area from Las Vegas, NV when I was a young girl, we had no immediate family here. The family we did have was distant and even further removed as the years passed. When my parents left this life I was alone.

I soon sank into a deep depression and sought therapy. It lasted a month at best because I could not afford the copayments on top of my other responsibilities. That was part of the reason I decided to start med school that August. In my mind, it promised to consume my lonely hours and be my therapy. Besides, I knew my parents Michael and Lauren Thompson would not want it any other way.

The day I started school fate reared its unpredictable head again in my life. I found what would end up being temporary solace in a chance meeting with Professor Jay Clark, as I was running late for a Biology course that beautiful Monday morning.

With an average height, medium build, and a milky white complexion, Jay was unlike any of my previous love interests. I had never dated outside of my race and was normally attracted to tall slightly husky men. This encounter would be a change in more ways than I counted on.

Although 15 years my senior, we had a lot in common. Like me Jay had lost both parents tragically, a mother to breast cancer many years prior and a father to a boating accident in the waters of the Potomac just a few short years ago. Both left a small fortune behind in the form of massive insurance policies. Instead of quitting, Jay continued teaching but lived a rather lavish lifestyle dining at the finest restaurants and shopping at the trendiest and most elite boutiques in the city.

Soon after dating, Jay took the reigns over my financial dilemma and ensured all of my bills were paid in full each month. I did not want for a thing. Soon after, I quit my job at the lab as well under Jay's advisement.

"No woman of mines will ever have to work a miniscule job," were the words that consumed my memory.

Sitting here today looking at the new round of bruises my face endured, I wondered if that was the true root of why I had stayed so long and if so what did that make me? A gold digging whore was all my mind could formulate as I cleaned up the mess around me and wept for what seemed like the millionth time in the past year and a half. My parents would be far from proud.

******

"Happy Birthday Karrine," Jay whispered in my ear for what I believed to be the second time as I tried my best to sit up and focus.

It can't be, I thought as I stretched and yawned. The new round of pain caused me to whence. I immediately grabbed my left cheek and moaned.

The vodka and cranberry I gulped down the day before, after removing myself from the barricaded bathroom, did nothing for the pain that was left over from the pummeling I received that day. In fact I was feeling additional anguish from the alcohol induced hangover now coupled with the swelling in my left eye. Given the facts, it was another year of life I secretly wished many times over would end rather than be celebrated.

"Be easy baby," Jay said with a smile while picking up a large neatly wrapped brown and cream box with a huge white bow from the side of the bed and handing it to me.

I fingered the large bow on the present while trying my best to focus out of my good eye, taking note of Jay's cheerful demeanor as I opened the gift. It was the usual song and dance as if nothing ever happened. Inside the beautifully wrapped box rested a large Louis Vuitton handbag and two tickets.

"Thank you," I said with mustered up excitement while trying my best to fake a smile and not awaken the beast I knew was lurking behind my lover's fake façade and eagerly looking for an excuse to break free.

The truth was I wanted to toss Jay and the gift out of the window. I had become accustomed to the routine and the fact that it was my birthday only made the gift box larger and its contents more extravagant.

"The tickets are round trip tickets for you and me to celebrate your birthday in Hawaii," Jay said in a matter of fact tone as if right on cue.

"We are leaving tonight," were the final words that fell on my ears.

Jay knew I hated celebrations of any kind since my parent's de-mise, not to mention my birthday, which also ironically marked what would have been their anniversary. Although the trip may have been a gesture to try to smooth over the previous day's events, the fact that my birthday and my parent's anniversary were tied to it did nothing for the cause this time around. I wasn't going.

"I can't," I mumbled and lowered my head.

"Karrine? Honey, if this is about yesterday, I am sorry sweetheart and I promise I will never ever react that way again. I was stressed from a long day…" Jay started, continuing the routine.

"Stop it," I interjected a few octaves higher than I intended.

"I do not like celebrations and this one happens to be my parent's anniversary as well," I said my voice beginning to waver.

"I am not going," I concluded and tossed the box on the floor.

"Really? Karrine you need to stop bitching and get over it!" Jay practically yelled with beads of sweat now forming.

SMACK!

I watched Jay's eyes grow large with shock as she grabbed her left cheek and arose from her position on the bed in front of me traces of her femininity finally showing.

For the first time in our relationship, I struck Jasmine Clark with a thunderous force that even shocked me as I stumbled to my feet as well.

"Bitch! I can't believe you hit me!" She screamed as she reached out with open palms aimed at my neck.

Adrenaline now surging through my body, I used all of the strength I could muster in my 5'10" frame to my advantage and blocked her hands sending her smaller body into an unexpected 180 spin. Stunned by my aggressiveness she lost her footing and hit the floor with a small thud. She then grabbed my ankle, pulling me down with her, and the fight began.

Bits and pieces of my life flashed before me, including my parents final words of pride, as everything around me became a blur. I was losing the fight of my life as she straddled and choked me. In a final attempt to win the battle, I reached for the lamp on the nightstand and landed it on her head; knocking her out cold. I freed myself from her stiff body and began coughing from the lack of oxygen my lungs were hungry for. I then reached for the phone and achieved another first as I dialed the numbers 9-1-1.

That birthday and what would have been my lovely parents Mi-chael and Lauren Thompson's anniversary marked a turn of events for me. I made a vow from that day forth to love myself first and to never let circumstances drive me to the point of self hatred or destruction.

With the help of friends I thought I pushed out of my life, I would seek professional therapy again amidst my pain. In time, I would begin the process of healing, which included first removing Jay from the equation and finally beginning to cope with the events that transpired in the months after my parent's death.

The revelation that I was allowed to grieve and heal in my own time was the greatest feeling I had since the tragedy and my turning to a woman in hopes of easing my pain. The notion that love, no matter the package, equaled understanding was liberating. Knowing love did not have to hurt was in fact, the sweetest hangover.

Kiexiza Rodriquez

Kiexiza Rodriquez, is the eldest of 11, the mother of 4, and currently resides in Virginia with her fiancée and her youngest two children. She is the Executive Director at DiamondStar Entertainment and a published author. Her first release, entitled "Beautiful" is the first in the "Beautiful Series," which is a 5 part book sequel that will delve into more than just romance, but also has aspects of mystery and an overall inspirational message.

Kiexiza aspires to do more than tell a mere, entertaining story with her novels. She desires to move people and inspire them to see the deep picture behind her characters; why they do what they do and end up where they do on life's journey? She hopes that by revealing a bit of herself and her life in her stories, maybe she can help someone not go through some of the pain she had to endure.

WHY I WROTE:

I decided to contribute to this anthology, not only because I am co-founder along with Elizabeth Funderbirk, but because as a victim I remember feeling alone. I remember wondering if anyone really understood how I felt, or did they all just blame me? I remember being a child wishing someone would stop my father from beating my step-mother. I wished my mother wouldn't shove soap down our throats, or beat us with hangers, and extension cords. It is my hope that a woman, man or child going through any kind of abuse can read this and discovers that there are others that understand. I pray that every person who reads this book will donate, support and spread the word on SLTL's mission to support the foundations that give these families a new start.

LINKS:
www.kiexizarodriquez.webs.com
www.facebook.com/authorkiexizarodriquez
www.twitter.com/Authorkiexiza
www.kiexizarodriquez.wordpress.com
www.blogtalkradio.com/tonynkieshow
www.diamondstarentertainment.webs.com

A Victim

Dinner was on time,
But he came home late.
The house was clean,
but lil John Jr dropped a bean on the floor
as he was cleaning his plate.
None of the things I do all day
matter...
Not one of the good things I did,
does he care to see,
All he walked in and saw
was the bean on the floor,
and no steam from his plate
filling the air...

Screams became blows
as I try to plead.
Blows became screams
as he tells me he doesn't care.
Why is this how he loves me,
when I give him my world?
Why can't I just leave,
instead of kissing the floor?

My children think it's my fault,
"why can't you just do right,
why can't you fold his clothes,
and cook the food he likes?"
They don't see me
for who I really am.
I'm not their loving doting mother
the one who goes to all their games
and recitals,
I'm the mistake, their father wishes he never
made...

Saving Lives Through Lit

So much makeup on my dresser,
in my purse,
I should own stock and be a millionaire.
Not even my family comes around
he's turned everyone against me..

I hear his car in the drive way
and cringe knowing something will be wrong,
no matter how much I try
I know fists will be thrown.
don't question him,
don't object,
do everything 100% correct,
every time all the time,
or his wrath my body will feel.
When did this idea I wonder
of love get instilled in him?

Balled up in a corner
as he kicks the life out of me,
I thought he would be happy
maybe go easy for once,
hell he had no problem
when he held me down
to get inside of me...
the news of another him,
another mouth to feed,
sends him on a rampage
that thankfully
my neighbors this time hear.

Laying in sterile room
bloody and beaten,
I feel my life draining from me.
People whisper quietly thinking I can't hear
"She's been here before, why oh why does she stay?"
and suddenly my soul feels ashamed

Voices Behind the Tears

A firm hand on my shoulder
makes me wince in pain
"you better not open you F****ng mouth"
I hear him exclaim
as if they don't know he's the one
there's not a door in the world
that can cause THIS much damage.

I close my eyes praying to die
I can't do this
can't go back to that house
God please just let me die
I hear myself scream inside.

Another hand I feel
much smaller and gentler than his
no words are spoken but I can hear
someone as they breathe
as moistness engulfs my hand.
"Mommy please take me with you"
I hear my daughter's tiny voice say,
"if you die, will he beat me, next?
Please Mommy take me with you!"
Then I hear him drag her away...

Something in me stirs
I guess something snaps
Something in me knows
I have to wake up
I've got come back
I've got to get out of this bed
and protect my children...

A light has been switched on
that I will never turn off...
no longer will I be his bag
to beat upon,

no longer will I be the weak one...
I wonder how he will react
the first time I smack his ass back?

"Something's have got to change round here"
No longer will I play his victim...
for the first time in a long time i smile
even though I know, no one can see it
I can feel it..
and it feels good.

Voices Behind the Tears

Can You See Me?

What do you see when you look at me?
Can you see what sits behind the smiles,
behind the facade?
Can you see the pain, the rain, the storms,
this body has been through?

Can you see behind my eyes?
Can you see the me I refuse to let show,
for fear you won't love me...
the real broken me?

My dreams, my aspirations
Hopes and desires...
They slip out.
Spill out onto an awaiting world
Can you see my joy?
Can you feel my excitement?
Can you feel my soul tremble,
At the thought of what Might be?

The thought that happiness might be
Just one step away..
And really happen for me...

Can you see?
Can you see the real me...
Behind what I allow you to see?

And can you Love this me?

Behind the Eye of Kie Rodriquez
@2011
www.kiexizarodriquez.webs.com

This Road

There was a time when I
Prayed for love,
When I prayed for the rain to end,
For this life so full of hurt
to be more than the same.

There was a time
When punches and bruises
Screams and yells,
Were a common place.
A time when I never thought
God knew or cared
For my tears

I shed.

There was a time
When my body laid
Bloody and sore
My insides ached and yearned
For peace...
But there was no release.

One time, so drunk I knew not how I got home

Voices Behind the Tears

One time, so scared, as a blade caressed my neck,

Shhhh, was all I heard

One time, tears rolled down my face,

as he smiled, oblivious at my attempts to push him off me.

Did he know he was hurting me,

as he kissed me, told me he loved me?

And rolled over and went to sleep...

How many times can I go down this road

So empty, full of hurt at every turn?

Memory lane...

Why can't I shake this pain?

There was a time

When I thought I found my forever after

In your embrace.

I haven't felt your arms around me in weeks.

There was a time when

Just a look from you made me want to jump

All over you,

you no longer look at me the same...

Our backs now talk to each other as we sleep

Saving Lives Through Lit

Our flesh yearns for companionship
yet our bodies never meet
Is our Love, is fading
What happened, it's too soon.
Too soon for this happy ever after to be

Devoured, destroyed...

Too much, I don't understand.
Too many words that cut me,
That cut you. How can we recover?
Is this the wrong road?
Were we blinded to the signs?
Or are we blinded
to the turns to get back on track?

This road is dark

Dismal

Cold

Alone

There was a time
I thought this feeling was gone
But now somehow...
It has returned!

Kie 2011

Joyce Oscar

Growing up in Memphis Tennessee, Joyce Oscar seems to have always had stories and rhymes in her head. Many days she would sit in her room writing song lyrics and later force her neighborhood friends to sing them. By the time she was in high school her love for reading and writing had become stronger. She attributes her love for words and expression to one of her literature instructors at Hillcrest High School.

Throughout high school and beyond, Joyce has maintained many journals, but the journals that she wrote as an adult were the ones that gave her the inspiration for her first book of poetry, After Midnight: Love's Journey. She feels that poetry had the power to re-create the human experiences like, falling in love, losing love, facing death and disease and finding God.

In addition to being an author, Joyce is owner and CEO of Agaphe Publishing Group and CFO of Rever Entertainment. She hosts a monthly radio segment called the Lounge that airs on the LMB Network. A single mom, Joyce lives outside of Atlanta, Georgia with her two kids. She is an alumnus of the University of Memphis and Mercer University and holds a degree in both Accounting and Information Technology. She is also an advocate of community service and volunteers with community organizations such as The Atlanta All-Stars Talent Network, The Pebblebrook Jr. Falcon Track Team, and the Pebblebrook Beta Phi Step Team.

WHY I WROTE:

"I write because if I cry, someone might see my pain...."
Smiling all the time was a hard but to me it was a necessity. However, there were so many times I was afraid that people would see beyond my smiles, beyond my stories of bliss. Of course, most of them were lies. I remember sitting on the edge of the bed watching him sleep. There was so much going on in my heart and head that I could hardly think straight. I HATED him! Even more, I hated myself for what I was allowing myself to go through. I wanted him out of my life, but as he so often told me, "only death would tear us apart". I believed him and I was afraid. One day I decided that death was the only way, but it wouldn't be mine. As I mixed the powdery substance and added it to his meal, a voice in the midst said "Be strong and courageous. Do not fear or be in dread of them, for it is the LORD your God who goes with you. He will not leave you or forsake you." I believed the voice and I was no longer afraid.

I wanted to be a part of this anthology because just like me, so many are afraid to JUST LEAVE. I pray that my story and my poetry will touch on someone's heart and help them to see that it's definitely possible to just walk away.

LINKS:
www.agaphepublishing.com
www.joyceoscar.com
www.lmbnetwork.com
info@agaphepublishing.com

The Faces of Me

There goes the woman in the fur coat
She's smiling and looking divine.
"It's a gift from my husband," she said.
"He gave it to me last night"
There goes the woman with the diamond ring
It glistens exquisitely in the light.
"It's an unexpected gift from my boyfriend,
He gave it to me last night"
I saw the woman with the new car,
It was perfect, shiny and bright.
"My husband surprised me with it," she exclaimed!
"He gave it to me last night"

Remember the woman with the beautiful kids,
She protected them with all of her might.
Now they'll have to protect themselves,
Their father killed her last night.

In His Solitude

as the sun begins to fade
and the hallow moon begins to rise
within the indigo hues of nightfall
a little boy rests his weary eyes.
somewhere in the city
his lost soul seeks its place
it seeks a place of comfort
to end his struggling race.
you see today wasn't a good day
not a good day at all
because today was the day
that his many faces began to fall.
hands of steel, fists of fire
it feels like a freight train
running over his head.
he begs and pleads, but it doesn't stop
he tries to remember what he did.
"I'll beat it out of you,
I'll make you right, and just you watch and see.
I'll make you right once and for all
you'll never embarrass me!"
who is this man, the man he loves
the one that he calls Dad
it has to be a stranger, this can't be him.
he wonders why he's so mad.
he reaches out for his mother
but she wasn't there
it was a useless try.
his body is in pain,
his mind is confused
but he's determined not to cry.
"why me" he yells,
"what did I do to deserve such scorn?"
with flaring eyes of aversion,
dad callously answered,

Voices Behind the Tears

"you were born."
his mind wanders and takes a journey
it goes to a place where he can be free,
he doesn't have to pretend
he doesn't have to hide
he doesn't have to conceal the feelings inside.
"I am what I am", he wanted to say.
"why can't you just love me for me"?
he wanted to yell it to the top of his lungs
but instead he just ran away.
so as the hallow moon begins to fade
and the morning sun begins to rise
now a man, no longer a boy
he opens his rejuvenated eyes.
somewhere in the city
his soul has found its place
it's found a place of comfort
to end life's struggling race.
each day from now on will be a good day
there will be no more dark clouds
he's standing tall, He's standing strong
and he's standing proud.
for his soul is no longer lost
it's found a resting place
it's found a place of comfort
in the arms of God's saving grace.

Last Night

I cried last night but I can't remember why
But I do remember the river
flowing from my eyes
the taste of pain upon my cheeks
and chin
and the destruction and anguish
of my soul within
I cried last night but I can't remember why
But I do remember the gloom filled clouds
as they toured my sky
the thunderous voice of hateful words
being said
the electric volts
as I protected my head
I cried last night but I can't remember why
But I do remember the daunting sounds
of the sirens near-by
the clank of the doors as they opened
for my arrival
and the cries of the babes
sobbing for my survival
I cried last night…
Oh yea… now I remember why
they were tears of joy
as he was carried out of my life
no more hiding behind
lenses and lies
no more seclusion,
my world I no longer despise.

When You Look at Me

What do you see when you look at me
the sadness in my eyes,
the distress in my face
the falseness of my smile
or the depression in my waist?
Do you see the struggle in my walk
when I come thru the door,
or feel the hurt in my voice
when I can't take any more?
Do you understand the cries in the night
after everyone is in bed?
Can you hear the confusion of the many voices
yelling in my head?
Do you know the relief I feel
when these walls aren't around?
Do you know who peace is
and why he can't be found…
for me that is

C. Highsmith-Hooks

    C. Highsmith-Hooks has been writing since she could hold a pencil. Her early works consisted of poetry and short stories. Her first book, "The Soul of a Black Woman: From a Whisper to a Shout," was published in 2002. The collection of poetry earned her a mention in Literary Divas: The Top 100+ Most Admired African-American Women in Literature, a 2006 Amber Books Publication.

    Earlier this year, more poems were published in The Poetic Child anthology, an Inner Child Publication compiled by William S. Peters Sr. and the poet known as Poetically Spoken aka S-cents.

    Born on the east coast, C. Highsmith-Hooks is the proud mother of one son. These days, she works a traditional 9 to 5 until the pen pays her bills. When she's not writing, she enjoys watching crime thrillers, traveling, and surfing the internet.

    C. Highsmith-Hooks is currently working on several novels, a few anthologies, and four screenplays. She lives in Las Vegas.

WHY I WROTE:

I was moved to participate in this project because I have seen domestic violence all around me for my entire life. Never a victim myself, I have friends and family who experienced it daily. So for me, the topic has never been far from my heart.

It's very important that we all speak out against it because while it's going on, it's hard for the victims to speak out. They're too busy fighting to stay alive-save themselves and their children. So we are their voices, their strength. Perhaps if they know they're not alone, they will fight to become survivors and encourage others with their example.

LINKS:
http://chighsmithhooks.webs.com/

And So I Speak

I see her-
battered and bruised
by familiar hands;
wearing shades on a day
when there is no sun.
Her dark eyes matching
her chopped-off hair.
She waves.
And so I speak.
Her deep stare
reminds me
of someone I knew.
Her eyes tell a story
that her lips never will-
Her silent tears
are a cry for help,
but help never comes.

And so I speak.
"Did he do this?
Why don't you leave?"
She says she can't-
no place to go.
He beats her that night
for talking to me.
When I see her again,
she hangs her head.

And so I speak.

In the hospital room,
her unhealed scars
and broken bones
still show the signs.

Saving Lives Through Lit

The doctor asks
if she's afraid.
She opens her mouth;
only whispers escape.

And so I speak.
I see her
wearing Sunday's best;
her blackened eyes
now closed for good.
I wipe her tears,
then touch her hand.
No one to mourn
or say kind words-

And so… I speak.

~C. Highsmith Hooks

Charron Monaye

As a child, Charron Monaye always relied on her pencil and notebook as a way of releasing her happiest moments, deepest secrets, and hidden desires without judgment. Her journal entries soon became poetic pieces she would later recite in front of crowds. At age 11, Charron Monaye made her first poetic debut at the United Negro College Fund's Awards Banquet, where she recited her award-winning poem "ALONE", which made Charron Monaye realize her gift from God was writing and it was time for her to pursue it.

After dealing with anxiety and heart-related health issues in her twenties, she decided it was important to share her story with women worldwide. In October of 2010, she was introduced with Londa B. of Purposeful Publishing and Media Services and decided to publish her thoughts, feelings, and emotions in her book entitled, "My Side of the Story". On February 1, 2011, "My Side of the Story" was birthed and released to the world, making this Charron Monaye's first published book of poetry and a dream of true. Tackling topics that include love, relationships, tragedy and triumphs makes this book of poetry unique and inspirational, not only women of color but all women who have battled with emotional losses, life changing health issues, but survived. Her decision to survive and reclaim is spotlighted in her heartfelt poetic verses throughout the book. This book is not just her testimony, but it is her own advice manual for all.

Charron Monaye currently resides in Philadelphia, PA with her two sons. Charron is a member of Zeta Phi Beta Sorority, Inc. and Order of Eastern Star, Ruth Chapter #66 PHA. Her educational background includes a BA in Political Science from West Chester University of Pennsylvania, Paralegal Certificate from Washington Learning Institute and a Masters in Public Administration from DeVry University.

WHY I WROTE:

Being a survivor of Domestic Violence, this book really warmed my heart. Many women and men who are victims of this crime often times hide or remain quiet in fear of judgment, ridicule, or opinions casted that only sheds more hurt. My testimony and survival from Domestic Violence can be found in my book of poetry entitled "My Side of the Story" (available now on Amazon.com). My abuse was not physical, but emotional and mental, thus creating a confused and lost child who had no hope or direction, only seeing what he thought was right. After 2 heart attacks and countless anxiety attacks, the doctors gave me months, but after seeing my 2 children crying and asking, "Mommy are you going to be okay", I knew then, my road was life and survival was my direction. So with this, I feel honored and a great asset to this project because not only can my poetry heal someone else, they continue to remind me of what mistakes not to do again."

LINKS:
www.charronmonaye.com
charron.monaye@gmail.com

Believe

It takes strength
To handle all the abuse I did
And still smile

It takes power
To take back what was stolen from me
And still have the desire to give

It takes determination
To keep striving for success
When I am forced to walk alone

It takes pride
To be happy for what I have
I worked hard for it; nothing was ever given to me

It takes life
To show you your mistakes
But maturity to learn from them

It takes friends
To not only guide you through the fire
But walk through it with you hand in hand

It takes family
To support you in everything
No matter how many times you fail

But it is by God's Grace and Mercy
That you have every element needed to walk this journey
It's Him who gave you
Strength, Power, Determination, Pride, Life, Friends, and Family
So give thanks, send praise
Your journey is destined for you and only you
But it takes you to believe

Still Standing

Now that you see that I could make it without you
How does that make you feel?
You assumed that your absence would destroy me
That your good bye would injure my spirit,
Keep me from seeing
What my God had in store for me

You just knew my existence would crumble
Without you
I had no direction, no understanding of what I had to do
But the pain you left is what I used to guide me
Your memories gave me the energy to make it through
To show you that it was never you that gave me the life
You thought you took from me,
the day you left It was me and I owe me everything
that you did not appreciate
So
I am here to profess that unlike you, I am supreme and
Most Importantly
Still Standing.

Learn to Love

If someone wants to walk out of your life
Let them go
I know it hurts, it causes pain inside
But learning to love you is the only cure
Learn to love yourself
You are the root of your happiness
All things are possible
Don't hold onto people who want to be free
You should know that everyone has somewhere
They would rather be
It may hurt for a minute, but that too shall pass
You need to learn to love you
First, never last

Never give 110% of yourself
When there is no security that you will get it back
It's nothing you can do if that man you love, doesn't love you
There are other fish in the sea
Get the longest rod, freshest bait
Until you find someone who can be yours forever
But before you do that, I want you to recognize
That you are the gem in your life
The only person who knows how to love you right
Who knows how to
Make your light shine bright
Who can wipe your tears
And know that tomorrow everything will be alright
I know you want a man
But love and respect you first
It starts with you
So before you find someone to love
Learn to Love you

Last Night

Last night
I cried my last tear
I dreamt my last dream
I throw away all the memories
Everything which connects me to you is gone
There is nothing left so your power can't be reproduced
I won't tolerate the disrespect
You can't make me bow down to your orders
There is no way I can conform to your demands
When you have no clue or idea, what it really means to be my man
I deserve better
I will not settle for anything less
You can say what you want
You can scream and yell all you please
But today was your last opportunity to say anything else to me
I have nothing else to give
Won't be wasting any more of my time
You don't appreciate me, never have
I can't give you what you don't want
So the buck stops now
I'm done with you
Out of my life is where you are about to be
Last night I have let you go
Just like you did me
So last night was the last night I would ever share another thought
About you and me

Survival

My strength shows my struggle
My bloodshed shows my battles
My broken bones show my injuries
My smile shows my pleasure in spite of
My pain shows that I am still human
My broken heart shows that everyone isn't true
My imperfections show that I am not perfect
My drive shows that I keep it moving no matter what
My corns show there is no stopping me now
My determination shows that I "Can't stop, Won't stop"
My testimony shows that my life isn't much different from yours
My beauty shows that I come from a line of elegance
My sexiness shows that I am a woman
My timberlands show that I am not ghetto, but straight hood
My divorce papers show that I did give love a try
My pot belly shows that I am a great mother
But
The mere fact that my life hasn't stopped
Shows that I have survived!!!

Taquila Thompson

Taquila Thompson is a 22 year old single mother. At age fourteen she started to write poems as a hobby but after she gave birth to her first daughter, at age seventeen, she decided that she would pursue writing full time. She is now a mother of two with her first children's series being released. It is entitled "Not Your Ordinary Family." She was inspired to write the series from her own experience of growing up with a father in prison and by watching her daughter go through the same situation. So she decided to embrace it and let other families know that they are not alone. She's overcome a lot in her life and she just wants to touch the world one person at a time.

WHY I WROTE:

I wanted to write because I was a victim of Domestic Violence myself and I never thought that it would happen to me. When it did I let it happen one more time before I finally realized that he would kill me before something changed. I want my story to help others realize that this is not okay and that you do have a voice.

LINKS:
www.facebook.com/authoresstaquilat
www.facebook.com/notyourordinaryfamilyseries

Free to be me

I saw the room turning black
I could barely catch my breath
I kept hearing him say, "Don't make me kill you bitch!"
I was about to give into the darkness
Let it completely take my body over because
I was starting to feel at peace
When I heard the soft cry of my daughter
I forgot that she was around and I just knew he was going to kill me right in front of her
I started to fight back but it was no use
Then he finally let go
He had fire in his eyes and I had sorrow in mine
I picked up my daughter to dress her so we could go
Then he started talking non-sense to me saying
that I was never going to be anything
That I was nothing but a bitch and I had no heart
I looked at him and something snapped inside of me
I stood up and started swinging on him as hard as I could
I wanted to hurt him like how he hurt me
I wanted him to feel everything he ever put me through
Then once again I heard my daughter crying so I picked her up and started to rock her
He then took that opportunity to hit me again
He started punching me on the side of my head and I covered myself and our child up
She started crying harder I don't know if he hit her or not
But at that very moment I knew this had to end
I didn't want my child to think that this was okay
I didn't want her to believe that a man putting his hands on a woman was a good thing because all that means is that he's a punk
I didn't want this cycle to continue on through her
And I didn't want to end up on my own episode of snapped because I was too afraid to walk away
I wasn't going to allow the hate I had built up towards him take away my freedom and my power as a woman
I was no longer going to let him belittle me

and make me feel as though I was worthless
That I was incapable of finding true love
So I did what my heart told me to do
I filed a police report and took my child and never looked back
I live my life to the fullest not worrying about having hands closed
around my neck or a black eye to cover up

I'm free to be

Latisha N. Patterson

A force to be reckoned with in the urban literary world, Latisha N. Patterson comes onto the scene with years of writing under her belt. The author of Airing Out Dirty Laundry, Patterson pushes through the door of opportunity with her motto, "can't stop, won't stop", and hasn't ceased to impress with her no-nonsense writing style.

Patterson's debut fictional novel, Airing Out Dirty Laundry, eases the reader in and out of erotica by intertwining real-life situations with love-hate characters who are forced to face skeletons in their closets. Inspired by events in her own life, Patterson's Airing Out Dirty Laundry describes the effects of long-term relationships riddled with secrets.

Born, raised and living in Richmond, Virginia, Patterson began writing in high school, with a focus on poetry and short stories. A passion for turning her imagination into literature for the world to see, has led her to launching a career in 2007, which promises to earn her the title of "It Girl" among her novel-writing peers. She still makes time for formal education, having already earned an Asso-ciate's Degree in Business Management, and currently pursuing a bachelor's Degree in Business Administration with a concentration in marketing. Latisha is the doting mom of two daughters, Mikiya age 12 and Tayanna age 10.

WHY I WROTE:

I think this is a great cause and I wanted to participate because I am a survivor of domestic violence. I was involved in a five year relationship that was abusive. I am proud to say that I am a survivor and I made it out alive. I want to raise awareness and give hope to those going through a similar situation and I want them know that there is a way out. It is not something to be ashamed of because plenty of people are going through it or have been through it. I hope to be an inspiration for others.

LINKS:
FMI: www.latishapatterson.com
Facebook: www.facebook.com/novelsbylatisha
Email: info@latishapatterson.com

A Different Kind of Love by Latisha Patterson

Elise

I was on my knees saying a prayer when my phone started ring-ing. I jumped up and ran to the kitchen snatching the cordless phone off the base. "Hello"

"Hey, girl I haven't talked to you in a while. How is everything going?" Trina asked in her bubbly over excited voice.

"I'm okay, just a lil bored. What's up with you? Why are you so happy?"

"I got a new job and I'm going to be making major figures. Come help me celebrate. I'm going to the mall to buy some new corporate America suits. We can do shopping and lunch."

Wow! God does answer prayers fast because I was just praying someone would come rescue me from this tiny cold apartment. "Congratulations, boo! Sure come get me. I should be ready in about thirty minutes but I can't stay out too long."

"Yeah, yeah I know. You have to be home before Chas gets off work. I'm leaving out now. See you in a few."

Trina knew I had to be home before Chas got home but she didn't know what would happen if I didn't make it on time. Trina is my best friend and I've known her for almost a year but it seems like we've been friends all our lives. Even though Trina is the only friend I have in Richmond I still keep parts of my relationship a secret. Trina wouldn't understand why I stay with Chas after she beats me.

I ran to the bedroom and grabbed some clothes out of the closet. I haven't been out of this apartment in weeks. My face just healed up from the punches Chas gave me last week for being disobedient. As long as I followed the rules everything was fine between us. As soon as I stepped out of line Chas felt it was her duty to put me in my place. As I lathered the Cucumber melon body wash on my loofah, I thought about me and Chas. When I first met her she was so sweet, caring, and loving. It felt so good to be myself around her. I know she had a rough childhood so I try to hang in there and pray things will get better. My once beautiful mocha skin has turned purple and black from all the bruises.

I hopped out the shower and brushed my teeth. Twisted my hair up in a bun and started to apply my makeup. I really don't like to wear makeup but I started wearing it to hide the bruises. As I was slipping on my shoes I heard a knock at the door. Damn, Trina is finally on time for once. I did a quick sprint to the door.

"Hey Trina; I can't believe you made it on time" I joked.

"Girl, I had to because I have so much to tell you and so many stores to grace my presence with."

"Well let's go. I'm ready!" I did a quick scan of the living room to make sure nothing was out of place then I locked the door behind me. I got into Trina's Camry and reclined the passenger seat a bit to get comfortable. "So tell me all about your new job." Trina was more than happy to give me the run down on her new job. I was trying to pay attention but my mind kept wondering what would happen if I didn't make it back home on time. Part of my prayers had been answered but the part about Chas not hitting me anymore had gone unanswered. I think I'm partly to blame because I choose to be with a woman instead of a man. Sometimes I think God is punishing me for being with Chas. For some reason I've never been attracted to boys. I never had a boyfriend growing up but no one thought it was weird because I was the preacher's kid. My father is Pastor Robertson of Mt. Olive Baptist church in Greenville, North Carolina. I wasn't allowed to date boys so I know my father would have had a fit if I told him I was gay. I was so happy when I graduated high school because it gave me a chance to get away from my family and be myself. My father agreed to let me go to college in Virginia because it was a great school. VCU was my first choice for college. I wanted to get away but still be close enough to drive home on weekends and holidays.

"Why are you so quiet Elise? What's on your mind?" Trina asked, once she noticed I slipped into another world.

"I'm just thinking about how things changed so fast. It seems like it was just yesterday when we were in the dorm together. Now you are going off to work your dream job and I'm a college dropout."

"Have you told your parents yet?"

"Hell no and I'm not going to! I will try again next semester. Chas said she will pay for me to take one class until I can get my financial aid back."

"Girl, you need to leave Chas ass alone. She is nothing but trouble. Since you met her your life has done nothing but go down a road of destruction. She got you smoking weed, drinking, popping pills, and missing classes. She's the reason you are suspended now." I knew everything Trina was saying was true and that is exactly why I never told her about Chas beating my ass. The real reason I miss classes is not because I'm high it's because of all the bruises to my face and body.

"I know Chas has her issues but I love her and she needs me. You know she doesn't have any family, they all disowned her. I'm all she got."

"Whatever, Elise… You need to start thinking about yourself for a change. Who did she have before she met you? Chas is a big girl. She will be fine without you just like she was fine before she met you. Just like you were so much better before you met her. I feel like it's my fault. I should have never let you go home with her that night." I could tell Trina was thinking about the night we went to this club called Colors. It's a gay club in downtown Richmond. Trina was my roommate when I lived on campus my first semester of college. Once I met Chas it was love at first sight and I moved in with her two weeks after we met. Trina said she didn't think it was a good idea but I ignored her. I didn't want to hear "I told you so" that's why I conveniently left details about my relationship out. I will never forget the night I met Chas. She was looking so good in her dark denim jeans and Timberland boots. She reminded me of Queen Latifah when she played Cleo in the movie set it off. Chas looked just like her especially when her hair was braided in cornrows straight back. Chas is what you call a stud. She forgets she's a girl sometimes and the way she beats my ass I forget as well. I looked at Trina in her eyes, "Everything will be alright. Chas and I will help each other get back on track. I don't smoke weed anymore and the pill popping is down to a minimum."

"Well I'm glad you are getting it together but I think there is no hope for Chas. Shit, she's twenty five years old and still stuck on stupid. She has no intentions of changing." I hate to admit it but I think Trina's right. On the ride home I tried not to act nervous but the clock in the car read 4:30pm. Chas gets off work at 4:00 p.m. but its Friday so she usually cashes her check and makes her little runs to the ABC store to pick up a bottle of Hennessey. Chas is what I call an alcoholic and when she drinks she gets violent. I think she inherited it from her father. Chas told me how her father used to beat up on her mom every time he got drunk. Then after he finished beating her he would come beat on Chas. Chas said she promised herself she would never let a man beat on her so she decided to be gay. The funny thing about it is she turned out to be just like her father. The man she hates so much. When we pulled up to my apartment I grabbed my purse and jumped out the car. "Thanks for the mall trip Trina. I'll check you later." I didn't even wait for her response. I slammed the car door and ran upstairs. I opened the door to the apartment and Chas was sitting on the sofa with her feet propped up on the coffee table drinking a beer. "So nice of you to come home… Where the fuck you been?" Chas said frowning up her face looking at me with disgust. She got up from the couch and walked up on me. "What the fuck is wrong with you Elise? You know you are supposed to be home cooking my dinner." Chas roared as she slapped me around the living room of our apartment.

    The neighbors were used to the constant arguing so no one even bothered to call the police anymore. I had become a human punching bag for Chas as if my name was changed to Everlast. I tried to explain but it was hard to while getting my face smashed in.

    "I just went out with Trina. I didn't mean any harm. All I did was go to the mall. Damn, I can't have any fun!" As soon as the last word escaped my mouth a foot to the gut is what I received.

    "Fun? What the fuck you mean you can't have any fun? Oh, so it's no fun being with me is that what you're trying to say?" Even though Chas was asking a thousand questions they all must have been rhetorical because I didn't dare say another word. Chas continued to kick me while I was down on the ground holding my abdomen from the kick I just received.

    After what seem like hours but was actually only five minutes Chas finally calmed down and stopped kicking me. Blood was pouring from my mouth and the tears only made my face hurt even worst. "I don't know why you can't just be the woman I need you to be. If you would just do what I tell you we could avoid all of this drama. Now get your ass up off the floor and clean yourself up. You're getting blood on my damn carpet."

    I struggled to stand to my feet but the ass whooping I just received made it damn near impossible. As I struggled to stand, shooting pains ripped through my stomach and back so I figured it would be easier to just crawl to the bathroom. I managed to wet a washcloth and wipe the blood from my hands and face. Finally I managed to stand up and look in the mirror. "Damn another black eye," I mumbled. I don't know how much more of this I can take. I try to be strong and hang in there thinking things will change but she never changes. I'm so tired of this shit. Plain sick and tired... I thought to myself.

"Hurry up and bring your ass in here and cook me something to eat. You know damn well you shouldn't have been out with that trick Trina anyway. I just got home from work and ain't shit in here on the stove." Chas yelled from the living room. She had sat back down on the couch to finish her beer. She flipped through the channels trying to find something to watch on TV.

"What would you like to eat dear?" I said in a condescending tone. I was not trying to have another fight. It was better just to kiss her ass and let her think she was in control.

"Whatever the fuck you plan on cooking and I don't want no bullshit either." Chas shouted never leaving the couch. Things had gotten so bad between us Chas even stopped apologizing for whooping my ass. She even stopped buying gifts. The first time things got out of hand Chas swore it would never happen again. She even bought gifts to make up for it and apologized repeatedly. Now she was to the point she didn't even feel bad after she beat my ass. I was to my breaking point. At this very moment I was tired; tired of having black eyes, tired of making up stories, tired of the mental abuse. Enough was enough. I slapped some pots and pans around then decided I wasn't taking Chas shit anymore. "Chas come in here and fix your own damn food, you big bitch!" I shouted. After the words escaped my mouth I knew I was treading on thin ice. I tried to fight Chas once before but I was no match for her strength. I'm 115 pounds wet with clothes on and only 5'4. I never had to fight a day in my life and here I was going up against a heavyweight champ.

"What the fuck you just say. I think I hit your ass too hard this time because you done lost your damn mind. Now I got to get off this couch after a hard day's work and kick your ass again. I swear bitches never learn." Chas hopped up off the couch and stormed into the kitchen but this time I was ready I held a cast iron frying pan in my hand and was ready for battle. "I'm tired of your shit Chas. You have turned into your worst nightmare, your father. I can't take this shit no more so come on with it." I was shaking uncontrollably and my heart was beating so fast you would have thought I just ran ten laps.

"Oh, so you want to rumble. You left the house with your lil hoe friend now you think you got balls. I dare you to hit me." Chas wasn't the least bit shaken by my sudden move to square off with her. "You ain't anything but a lil scared bitch. Now put that pan down before you make things worse than they need to be. I'm tired and I don't have time to play games with you, Elise." As I stood there with the skillet in my hand ready to beat her head in I looked into my girlfriend's eyes and saw a glimmer of hope. Her eyes said that she loved me and she never wanted to intentionally hurt me. I put the pan down and went to hug Chas. "Baby, I'm so sorry. I wouldn't ever hurt you. I just snapped for a moment you know I'm under a lot of pressure." I put my arms around her neck and kissed her chubby cheeks lightly. She returned the hug then she suddenly became stiff. I could smell the beer on her breath. Good thing she's not drinking Hennessey or that would have been my ass. As soon as the thought crossed my mind Chas pushed me off her all I could see was a pair of knuckles coming towards my eye. "Oh, so you think I'm like my father huh, my father. So now you want to throw that shit in my face. Well I'll show you how my father whipped my mother's ass. Then I'll show you how he whipped my ass!" Chas was shouting so loud spit was flying out of her mouth as she struck me over and over again with her fist. The last punch to my face knocked me into the stove and I hit my head. My head was throbbing so bad I couldn't even think. My life started to flash before my eyes. As my breathing began to become irregular and my eyes started to roll back I realize my prayers had finally been answered. I prayed for peace and for Chas to stop drinking. I didn't want her to hit me anymore. God did answer my prayers but it wasn't the way I thought it would be. Chas stopped drinking because she went to jail for killing me. I was at peace because I was no longer on earth. I was no longer living in hell and Chas no longer beat me because I was dead. I hope my death is not in vain. I want to leave a legacy. I want women to know that you need to love yourself more than you love another. I wish my life had gone a different course but if I can help someone else avoid the mistakes I made I will have died a happy woman. Now I'm truly at peace.

Chas

"Damn,damn,damn!" I can't believe this bitch made me kill her. I was walking around the kitchen pacing back in forth. I didn't know what to do. I kept thinking Elise was faking. She was just trying to scare me but after fifteen minutes of slapping her and throwing water in her face she never got up off the floor. I ran into the bathroom and got a small hand mirror and placed it under her nose. Damn, nothing! She wasn't breathing. I heard sirens so I peeped out of the window. Nosey ass neighbors must have called the police. I was high from the blunt I smoked earlier and drunk from the 40oz I was drinking. I couldn't think fast enough. Before I could make a move to clean up all this blood the police was knocking on the door. "Police! Open up. We got a call about a lot of screaming and noise. Open up!" I walked to the door and opened it. "What can I do for you officers?" I said with slurred words and tears in my eyes. I knew I was caught and I was going to jail. I killed the only girl that ever really loved me. "I did it officer. I killed my girlfriend. She's dead. She's really dead." The officer looked at me with a raised eyebrow, "Where is she?" he asked. I lead the officers into the kitchen where Elise's lifeless body was laying on the marble floor. "What happened?" The officer continued to ask me questions but I wouldn't respond. Shit, I already made a mistake and blurted out I killed her. I was not saying another word without speaking to a lawyer first. His partner checked for a pulse and confirmed she was dead. He called for a coroner on his radio while the other officer read me my rights and placed the hand cuffs on me.

After hiring a lawyer and pleading guilty to involuntary manslaughter I received fifteen years with five years suspended. This was the first time I ever been locked up and ten years is a long time but nothing will compare to the nightmares I have every night about Elise. If only I would have listened to her and got help for my drinking. I guess the apple doesn't fall too far from the tree because I ended up being just like my father. The man I tried so hard to forget about, I became him. It's too late for Elise but the least I could do to honor her memory is to seek help. I decided to join the drug and alcohol rehab group in prison. I even started talking to a counselor. Maybe I can get rid of some of these demons living deep down inside me. What happened that night still haunts me and I regret that things ever went that far. As the guard walked around to do the final count for the night and to call lights out I got down on my knees and begin to pray. "Lord, please forgive me for all my sins. I never meant to kill Elise. I hope she is in a better place. Lord, please guide me in the right direction and use me to prevent others from following my footsteps. Amen

Mashawn Mickles

My name is Mashawn Mickels. I was born in Ft. Benning, Georgia, yet raised around the world. My most recent stay was Columbus, GA, but I currently reside in Alexandria, VA. My passion is poetry. Because of that, I currently have two poetry books out titled "A Piece of Me" and "Sexual Seduction". I'm also working on a novel. I also provide personalized poems for weddings, birthdays and other various events. I've recently begun to add postcards to my line of products as well. In the near future I will finish up two more poetry books. One is titled "Road of Emotions". The other, well, I'm still working on it.

I have two books out as stated here and I'm currently finishing up books three and four. I've also added some postcards to my line of products. I am the CO-Owner and President of SBS Book Club which is based out of Columbus, GA. I'm looking to expand the club so we are 'meeting' through conference calls now.

WHY I WROTE:

This book is important to me because domestic violence happens all the time. Many people are so afraid to tell someone because they think no one will understand. I feel that it's very important for others to know and understand that others have been through that and many have come out on top. A lot of times, low self-esteem is involved and it just needs to be rebuilt.

LINKS:
MashawnMickels@yahoo.com
Mashawn.com
Facebook.com/MashawnThePoet
Facebook.com/SBSBookClub
SBSBOOKCLUB@yahoo.com

SECRETS & LIES

Each day I close my eyes
I hope not to wake up
Yet each morning
I start a new day
Another day of secrets
More lies to tell
More fears to face
However I'm grateful
Just to see another day
I close my eyes
Bow my head in prayer
Ask for knowledge and strength
To continue to move forward
Then comes the day
One punch too many
One threat too many
I make a decision to move on
No more bruises to cover up
No more lies to tell
Never to settle for less again
I stand tall today
Head held high
Now I know the truth
The real deal is evident
You don't love me
You don't even care about me
So this is the end of the road
Time for me to move on
No longer will I be second
Never again to be unimportant
No longer will I be your punching bag
Never again to deal with you
Your thoughts no longer faze me
Your feelings are no longer important
I'm not afraid of you anymore

Saving Lives Through Lit

It's now my time to shine
My time to light the roadway
Today it ends for you
Now it belongs to me
Never again
No more
Secrets Behind Closed Doors

Voices Behind the Tears

MY STATEMENT

What is my statement
What is my command

When I'm with you
My identity is lost
When I'm without you
I crave to be with you
Never have I understood this

With you I cry
Because I want out
Without you I cry
Because I want to be with you

You confuse me
Your actions complicate my thoughts
My mind says no more
My heart says one more time

One more time
Turns into another try
Never again
Remains to be seen

I want to be with you
But it hurts my body
I want to never be with you again
But it breaks my heart

Now I know
Which road to follow
Now I know
The truth within myself

No longer can I sit here
And let you hit me

Saving Lives Through Lit

No longer can I go on
And cover for your abusive ways

Today I stand my ground
My mind is made up
Today I make my exit for good
My thoughts are my own now

No more tears
You can make me cry
No more hurt
You can cause me

This is my statement
This is my command

Good Bye
Good Bye

Mashawn Mickels © Oct 2010

Meka Phoenix Carter

Tameika Raye'la Carter is a single mother of three beautiful daughters. She was born and raised in Springfield, Massachusetts. She is a graduate of the High School of Commerce class of 1993 and a graduate of Holyoke community college. She is no stranger to hard work being raised by a single mother of five children. She learned the importance of strength and endurance. She has been through many hardships that have brought her to the point where she is today. As a survivor of domestic violence and other areas of abuse, she decided to get into the Human Service field to help others who have been in similar situations as she faced in her past.

Tameika has prided herself in her role in helping various parents and youths to make positive changes in their lives. Receiving her degree in the Human Services field was a way for Tameika to give back to the community in a positive way and be that positive voice in the lives of youth, preventing them from making the same mistakes she made in her own past. The woman who gave Tameika the most influence and mentorship through this time would be Jane Gilman, the instructor at HCC who taught the "Helping Relations course. Through this powerful woman, Tameika learned the importance of life and how every experience happens for a reason, and how I was an important tool to help others by what I have gone through. Her presence is still felt in everyday life even though she is no longer with us in the physical form.

Tameika is presently holding the position as the Youth Programs Coordinator for Valley Opportunity Council a non-profit organization based out of Holyoke, Massachusetts. In this role, she coordinates activities and finds employment for at risk youth who participate in the program; as well as leads a team of staff whose efforts together bring about a successful program. Working hand in hand with other vendors giving youth in the community an opportunity to wet their feet in the workforce and learn responsibility.

WHY I WROTE:

I am a Rising Phoenix, and I was lucky enough to make it out of the Hell of, domestic violence. I have made a vow to do all I can through community work, my words and my art to help others know that they too can arise and become stronger and wiser despite the situations they may have been through. If sharing how I have risen and continue to rise can help even one person, I know my journey was not in vain.

LINKS:
www.facebook.com/tameika10
www.tameikacater.webs.com

Voices Behind the Tears

My Son

By: Tameika Carter

Mommy misses you more than you will ever know.
I never got to hold you or ever see you grow.

A part of me is missing every day of my life; the worst part is its painful; it cuts deeper than the sharpest knife.

Nothings the same without you here; your mamma is at a loss. All this pain inside me is killing me slowly; who would've known life's occurrences could be held this long and this much damage cause.

If I could see you once again, and not just in my dreams; then everything will be okay for once. I would go to the God's for one more chance in tears and on bended knee.

I'm afraid of loving and even more to be alone. The strength I have developed is too much sometimes; it weighs me down emotionally and at times I feel forlorn.

Come to me my angel and give your momma strength... I so need you right now my son; Cuz deeper I don't wanna sink.

I miss you more and more each day and I wish I could see you my baby boy. To hold you in my arms once more
would bring me so much joy.

Taking a deep breath now and swallowing my pride. I hold your presence close to my heart and it will never die. Know that as you look down on us from your heavenly thrown... you are LOVED and thoughts of you will do nothing but grow!!!

R.I.P
Joaquim
(Your momma will eternally love you)

Darkness

By: Tameika Carter

I'm blinded by the darkness, still searching for the light.
I want to believe you, but something isn't right.

The voice that's deep within me just doesn't want to let go.
I am lost in my confusion, but unable to let it show.

Starting in the beginning you were a dream come true. Now as time passes on I feel obsolete and can't get close to you.

I am reaching out to touch you; but you're so far away. The more of me I give to you, the more you go astray.

I thought I had a good thing; I guess I was just blinded by love. I thought I would one day be the one who would wear your ring.

But it seems to the side is where I have been shoved.
I won't allow this feeling to overcome me anymore. I'm moving forward now, never looking back as I walk through that door.

You have betrayed me with your secrets; you have cut me with your lies. What hurt the most is that I trusted you
with all I had and now I must say goodbye.

Only fools fall in love, isn't that how the saying goes, I let down my walls and defenses? Next time I know which path not to go.

I was consumed by tunnel vision, with only you on my mind.
You were consumed by your ego
and other things and somehow I got left behind.

I gave to you my heart and soul, the hardest thing to do. Now I'm lying cold and naked in the dark, with endless thoughts of you.
I have gotten trapped in this black hole not knowing what to do.

Voices Behind the Tears

Now the time has come to put this emptiness to rest.
I close my eyes and float away cuz the weight is lifted off my chest.

I take my last breath and bid the world goodbye. Now my time has come, it's time for the buried inner pain to finally rest and Die.

Back with a Vengeance

by Tameika Carter

I'm the fiery Phoenix...
Ever so beautiful with my fiery wings soaring high
and making my mark where every I go.

REBORN!!!
Only greatness is to come.

Safe under the wings of the Phoenix!
Immune to the burning flames as long as you stay by my side...
flying fast on the "journey" no more tears to cry,
no more reasons to keep it all inside.
I am free
Strength in numbers is what they say,
so come fly free with me and together we will go...
to unchartered lands where no one else will know.
Leaving behind the sadness and hurt
no more of this we'll know.

I hope you're ready for the ride...
for the "Phoenix" is ready to go.
Leaving behind me an ashy trail of baggage
not needed for this ride.
The REAL me is unveiled no more reason to hide.

2011 is the rebirth,
and from here on out
I'm strategically taking each moment in stride.

Together united as one.
Fitting perfectly like a glove.
A perfect bond of union
as seen in the eyes of GOD.
Two imperfect creatures
created perfectly, joined to fly as ONE.

Voices Behind the Tears

Two different species of bird
but powerful in their own right.
Flying side by side as equals
as we fly straight to the moon tonight.

The time for change is upon us and Here I STAND!!!

N.S. Ugezene

N.S. Ugezene is the author of Pascal's Life and Pantaegeous. He is currently working on his third novel slated to be released in the summer of 2012. He started his journey into fatherhood in July and marriage, in May and welcomes life as a family man. Lastly, he is pursuing his Bachelor's degree at Argosy University and is expecting to graduate in December of this year.

WHY I WROTE:

I would like to be part of this anthology to attempt to empower victims of domestic violence not to tolerate it and to also, be active in a cause that will change a bad aspect of our world.

LINKS:
www.facebook.com/NSUgezene
N.S. Ugezene, author http://stores.lulu.com/NSUgezene

Refuse To Be Rainy
By N.S. Ugezene

The night before was passion-
Full course meal, wine, strawberries, candlelight
Afterwards, the bedroom delight-
All part of a pattern and denial was executed by both parties
She wanted to be tart each day to escape
But the fear in her heart instructed her to avoid the rape
Battered, time and time again but she wouldn't LEAVE
Only for a few days at a friend's house then she returned
The sweet talk from her man made her putty in his hand-
With every backhand, he has control and she's more damaged
"Bitch! BITCH! You stupid bitch!"

The total humiliation and disrespect she tried to fight but couldn't-
She heard so much ranting

1st voice: "My brother would beat his fuckin' ass!"
2nd voice: "You need to leave him. He doesn't love you!"
3rd voice: "How many times are you gonna' let him beat you?"

This battered and bloody woman whose name is Rainy said,
"I know Charles means no harm. It's just me who has to do what he says. I know I upset him and I have to stop. You know? Drop my bad habits.
When he says make cabbage, I need to obey and make cabbage.
I shouldn't fight. The time I confronted him about the strip club,
I shoulda' said nothing and made him realize that love was HOME-"

2nd voice: "Stop! A man who loves you doesn't go out to strip clubs behind yo' back then beat you. He treats you like a whore and you let him. Call the cops so they can come get him."

1st voice: "Yeah girl! Don't let this nigga' run you! What you should do is have his ass killed!"

The venom spewed from friends and loved ones crossed her mind
But she still couldn't find the strength to leave-
Why couldn't she have listened to her mother's plea a long time ago?"
"Rainy, please leave," she said. "Before you end up dead."
Tears fell and those words contained genuine sorrow
But those words went in one ear and out the other
And she refused the help offered by her brother, because-
She didn't want there to be drama-
A year and a half of the relationship went by
She began telling the same people who tried to warn her that she's gonna' marry Charles-
They weren't happy about the news but wished her luck

Almost four years, and tears were shed because Rainy was dead
"Why didn't she just listen to us?" her sister Yolanda cried out.
She was badly beaten and shot in the head
Mr. Charles in Charge!!! At large! He ran away-
If she had done the same and kept in that way,
Perhaps, he would have learned how to treat a woman
But he saw his father abuse his mother so he felt it was right
He preferred being so wrong-
November 22, a horrible day for Rainy's family and now,
They can't get along because of what a violent man did

Whatever indifference you feel is justified-
Realize there's so many people dead inside-
They felt they could love and be loved but they were told lies
They may at times look strong on the outside but inside, they cry
Don't give the issue a cold shoulder but please do SPEAK-
Help the battered and verbally abused to be free!
Again, help them to be FREE! They should want WANT to be FREE.

Poetic Swag

Darius O'Neal Farrar is a 23 year old young man who has been through a lot in his lifetime. Being bullied and verbally abused and teased by other kids at a very young age had him at a state of being very angered all the time. Darius started writing poetry at the age of 18 to help him deal with the death of one of his favorite uncles and he's been writing ever since. The biggest thing that shifted his poetry life was the death of his grandparents. He took it extremely hard and with the death of many friends closely following, he once again took to his love for poetry to help express the way he felt. Poetry is one of Darius' many passions; writing for any reason and every season. Darius can turn a bunch of scrambled words into a beautifully written poem. Darius can write a poem about anything at any time. His writing style is very different from other poets and is extremely needed in the world today. Darius writes about issues and problems that have been occurring in this world for many years but people try and either hide them or don't want to talk about them. Darius tries his best to put God in his poems because he believes that not only can all problems be solved by talking to God, but all things can be done through Christ!

WHY I WROTE:

The reasons I submitted my poem and the reason I want to participate in this is because I believe that domestic violence is something that happens more frequently than people actually want to believe. I believe that domestic violence happens to males just as much as females and people do not want to accept that. And I want to get the word out that males get raped and molested just as much as females do too. I want to get the word out to the entire world that domestic violence, rape, and molestation happens, people die from it daily, and we will no longer stand for it.

LINKS:
www.facebook.com/darius.farrar
www.facebook.com/pages/Poetic-Swag/269869253039592
www.tagged.com/farrard87
www.twitter.com/PoeticSwag87
drs_farrar@yahoo.com

Voices Behind the Tears

Mr. Abusive

Standing in the mirror along
With a blacken eye and swollen face.
I recite these words to myself;
I Am Beautiful! I Am Worth Something!
I Am Not An Animal, I Am Indeed A Human Being!
Talking to my sister on the phone
Slurring my words...
'It's not his fault. It's my fault.
I shouldn't of upset him!
He loves me and I love him, I'm not leaving.'
With tears running down my face.
'Leave him, a real man doesn't hit women.'
Is all my sister ever says.
He is a real man, I know of that for sure.
He reminds me every night weather I want him to or not.
At first, I thought I would be able to change him.
Then, I thought he would stop after telling me he would.
But, now, it's coming to a point where the beatings are getting worse.
Name calling, physical assaults, spitting, biting.
Why do I feel like I'm beneath him?
Hell, what do I know?
I don't even know my own worth!
Well, I didn't until
I met this one man
Who called me beautiful.
He said, 'You're a beautiful ebony queen
Not a dog's chew toy.'
He showed me what
Unforced love feels like.
Here I am, not even realizing
That the abuse my man, Mr. Abusive, gives me
Caused more harm to me than just hurt feelings and broken bones.
His abuse caused mental fear
His abuse caused emotional stress
His abuse even caused spiritual detachment.
But being with this unidentified man

Has left me with feelings.
Feelings of something I could not get with Mr. Abusive.
He says, 'true love will not blacken your eyes
True love will not swell your face
Nor brake any bones in your body.'
So, Mr. Abusive doesn't have true love for you.
Leave him and get your life back.'
That's what he said to me
And for some reason, I think he is right.
So leaving him is what I must do.
Leaving him is what I'm going to do.
Trying to pack up my bags quickly
Without waking up Mr. Abusive.
I know he's gonna be mad if he's woken.
Too Late...
With a knife on my throat
And an abusive man
Holding it while calling me out my name
Makes me feel like an animal.
And that's exactly what went down.
I felt like a chicken about to be de-skinned.
'Bitch, 6 feet under is the only way you're leaving me'
Slicing my throat from ear to ear.
As I slowly fell to the floor
Which seemed as if I was falling in slow motion.
All I see is that beautiful face of
The one man who was kind to me.
He wasn't white, he wasn't black
He was the color of BEAUTIFUL!
All I could do was call out his name
And hoped and prayed he heard my cries.
Jesus! Jesus! Jesus!
I suddenly hit the floor
And with nothing less than a scratch.
Watching as the police took Mr. Abusive away
And a second chance granted in my favor.
Praying every night
Witnessing to some and testifying to others

Voices Behind the Tears

The mercy God has for us all
Are most of the activities I do now.
Going and helping both MEN and WOMEN
Who are now in my former shoes
Letting them know that out is where
They must go and God will help as well
As his son, Jesus...

A Man's Cry: I Wonder If She Even Cares...

I wonder if she even cares about me?
All this name calling is wearing and tearing on my internally
My confidence level has dropped and
My the respect I have for myself is lacking
You're not the person that should be doing this to me.
We started as family, I your nephew you my aunt
Then we shifted into you being my baby sister.
Now, all I ever do when I come over there is cry.
I wonder if she even cares that she's hurting me.
Calling me worthless, calling me a punk
Yelling at me commands of take your clothes off
Isn't my idea of auntie-nephew time.
Ripping off my clothes if I'm moving too slowly
Touching me and licking me and sucking me
On an area that mommy told me
Is the "bad person touch area"
Then after I start having funny feelings and white stuff shoots out
You all of a sudden turn the tables and
Lay on your back with your clothes off
Lay on your back with your legs spread wide
Yelling at me commands of stick your tongue out...
Yelling at me commands of put your tongue in here...
Yelling at me commands of suck this right here...
Then after it's all done with, making me take an hour's worth
Of bath-time and telling me
Now you know auntie loves you right?
So no one can know about this but you and me!!!
I wonder if she even cares about
The years of nightmares she's given me!
I wonder if she even cares that
Because of her, I don't want to do anything
Sexually with any female because it only reminds me
Of those babysitting times with auntie!
But that was then, this is now and I'm a grown ass man now.
Standing at 6 feet tall 234 lbs of pure muscle at the age of 34
Walking into the church getting ready to burry you

I take one last look into your coffin, these words I say to you...
I FORGIVE YOU! MAY GOD HAVE MERCY ON YOU!

Mahogani P.

Inspired by life's stresses, emotional abuse as well as physical abuse from past relationships, to experiencing being homeless and betrayal from family & friends, Mahogani P. found solace in writing. Her first novel, The Soul of Toya Daniels, received wide acclaim from her peers, family, friends and other Authors. Mahogani knew she was destined for greatness! She grew upon on the north side in Mount Vernon, NY where she was always judged as what you would say "a miss goody too shoes" because of where she lived. She never let that stop her from being a free spirit, or stunt her creativity. She attended Mount Vernon Public schools and graduated from Mount Vernon High School, in Mount Vernon New York. She later went on and attended Berkeley College, graduated with an Associate's Degree in Business.

"I laugh, I joke, I cry, I fall, I get angry, I get frustrated… I do all these things just like YOU! Yet, I found through music, writing and voice…I live to see another day! Drama tries to find me… my pen releases me. I love to motivate people to push themselves. I love to write to inspire others to think and have a voice, not just read the words. I speak to not only motivate thy self, but to pass blessings on to someone else. I am a mother of two wonderful children who are my reason for all that I do. "Life has been a blessing, and it has also been very, VERY interesting to say the least. With that being said, I will leave you with this... Faith is taking the first step even when you don't see the whole staircase."

Author of "Memoirs of a Blessed Diva" (A 30-Day Diary of inspiration) (Available on Kindle)

Radio Host of Koffi Lit Radio, Creator of DiVa Soul Ink Publica-tions

WHY I WROTE:

I wanted to participate in "Saving Lives Throuh Lit" because I have had abusive relationships, both emotional and physical. I've been homeless, without a job and have stayed with family to get back on my feet. Back in 2005, after having my second child, I started to write to release my thoughts and pain. This project not only speaks to my heart, but I believe in what it represents. I enjoy uplifting, motivating and inspiring others to have a voice no matter of their circumstances.

LINKS:
Email: divasoulink@gmail.com
Twitter:@mahogani_p
Facebook: www.facebook.com/authormahoganipettiford

Excerpt from "Sins Of Innocence"

Chapter 5
Shalae's secret

It was about 3 a.m. and he walked in as if nothing was wrong. Shalae could tell he had been drinking and smoking weed all night. He had a stench that she could smell from the couch, as he stumbled passed her and into the bathroom to wash up. He only washed up when he came in after being with another woman. He didn't even notice that she was half asleep on the couch. Shalae wanted to say something but the Dr. told her that she had to remain stress free in her first trimester.

"What's up Shae? I know you aren't sleep. Get the hell up and make me something to eat." Brian always demanded that she fix him something to eat when he came in. That's because after smoking blunts all night, he had the munchies.

"What's the matter, your other chic couldn't handle fixing you something to eat?" Shalae said, not missing a beat to Brian's com-ment. Now one thing about Shalae is her mouth was as sharp as her suits that she would wear to work. She was always getting slick by the mouth, mainly because she knew it would piss him off.

"What did you say to me? Don't you ever speak to me like that again! Now get me my food! Crazy bitch!" Brian with an open hand slapped her right across the face for her sarcastic response, sending Shalae clear across the living room floor. He made sure he always left a mark on her to remind her that he was in charge. Shalae should've expected that, because he was drunk and he would always hit her when she didn't move fast enough to serve him. But this time, she was going to give him exactly what he wanted and deserved.

"I'm going! But the next time you hit me like that, it will be your last!" Shalae yelled as she got up from the floor and ran to the bathroom to see her bruise.

Brian yelled from the living room, "Yea whatever Shae! How many times have you said that to me? I'm losing count! Go get your face fixed up, get my food and hurry the fuck up, a nigga is starving." Brian said this as he plunged into their cream leather couch that Shalae brought a few weeks ago with her bonus check.

Shalae walked past Brian and into the kitchen to heat up the spaghetti she made the night before. But this time she was going to add a little something extra just to show Brian that she wasn't playing his games any more. She was tired of the beatings, fighting, and she was running out of excuses at work as to why her eyes were always swollen. Shalae added some grated cheese on top of the spaghetti along with some other extra sharp ingredients...

"Shae! Shae! Don't make me come in there after you girl! Hurry up!" Brian said.

"I'm coming damn it!" Shalae shouted from the kitchen. As Shalae walked over to the couch, Brian was comfortable with his red and black Hanes boxers on watching the big 54' screen TV that she just bought. Shalae dare not even try to change the channel because that would result in a never ending battle with Brian's fist in her face. It was already 4 a.m. and Shale had to be gone by 6 a.m. to get to work on time. Shalae knew that after Brian ate his food, her morning would be a long one, but she didn't care. Shalae was tired of the bullshit and she had had enough.

"Here you go baby, and I'm sorry I took so long to heat it up. But here you go and your drink too. I am going to go to bed; you know I have to be up in a little while. I love you." Shalae said with a devilish grin on her face as she walked back to their bedroom.

"Yea...Yea... go ahead man, I'll be in there when I'm done. You better be ready too." Shalae knew that once he was finished eating he would try to have violent sex with her but she made sure that wouldn't happen.

As Shalae listened to Brian devour the spaghetti, she lay still in her bed waiting to hear the screams, but they never came. She peeked out the bedroom door to look in the mirror they had up in the living room that showed the reflection of who was sitting on the couch. He never touched his drink yet. "What was he waiting for?" He always went for the drink immediately after he finished his food. That was his routine. "Why was he changing up his routine now?" Just at that moment, her cell was going off...

"Hey Shalae, it's your wake up call. Time to rise and shine, it is 5 a.m. and you don't want to be late." The automated lady said on the other end as Shalae answered the phone. Shalae hated that morning wake up call. But her mother set it up for her just so she can keep tabs on her. Shalae had an alarm clock to wake her up. She had no more time to try to catch any type of sleep, it was time to go to work, plus she had to meet with her new Supervisor early, so she went into the bathroom to fix her face.

She got up and showered, putting on her favorite interview suit and then some flat shoes. Even though she was just a few weeks along, her clothes started to feel a little snug and her feet had been hurting a month prior to her finding out she was pregnant. So she wore some comfortable sneakers but packed her shoes in a separate gym bag just in case. As she headed towards the living room and past the couch, the TV was still playing so damn loud. He had fallen asleep, which meant he never touched his drink! So Shalae decided to leave it right there on the coffee table. At some point he will touch it, and he will know that she means business. Too bad she wouldn't be here to hear the screams.

Just like any other normal morning, she would always try real hard to wake him up to kiss him goodbye. It never worked. He was always drunk from the night before because he never knew what hit him. Shalae grabbed the keys to his truck off the coffee table, locked the door behind her and headed down the stairs to her car. At some point today, Shalae knew she would get a phone call from him or someone else.

As she headed to work, she kept thinking about her mom and when she would go through this routine when she was a little girl. Her dad would beat her daily for no reason at all. She thought Shalae never knew what was going on, but she did. Her mother would always look up at her from the floor with her fingers over her mouth and whisper, "shhhh." She didn't want him to come after Shalae. She was very afraid of her dad growing up. When he got drunk, all hell would be break loose.

Shalae's mom would try so hard not to get beat, but when she would be cooking dinner, she would get beat just for not answering a question loud enough, or looking at her dad the wrong way.

Shalae's dad had a real serious problem, but her mother loved him. Shalae never understood why she stayed, but now that she is in that same position, so she understands the fear. Shalae was extremely afraid of her fiancé, Brian. She just didn't have it in her to leave him. They did have some good times, but more bad than good ones. Shalae always thought to herself, "Someday this man is going to kill me… then what would her momma or her unborn child do without her.

"Come on!!! Move your damn car already!! People need to get to work!" Shalae hated taking this way to work. Traffic was always heavy at this time of morning on the bridge, but it was the only route to get to her job. Her job was only 25 minutes away from her house but you would think it was hours the way these people drive in the morning. As Shalae was walking through the parking lot into work, her mother called her, like she did every morning.

"Shalae, baby are you sure you are alright? Did you make it to work alright?"

"Yes, momma I did. I am okay. How are you doing? How is your arm?" Shalae had heard from her Aunt that her dad had broken her mother's arm a few days ago. Her mother never tells her Shalae these things because she knows Shalae would chastise her, as if Shalae didn't have her own life to worry about with Brian. Shalae always found what was really going on with her mother and father from her Aunt, because Shalae would always have to talk her Aunt out of killing her father with her bare hands.

"I take it your Auntie called you? She never minds her business! Well I am fine and well… you know your father. He doesn't mean it. He just has a lot on his mind." Shalae's mother said.

"Momma, they never mean it. They always have something on their mind. It usually winds up with them beating us. I'm sick of it! But I fixed Brian's ass this morning. He should be feeling my wrath in a few hours when he wakes up." Shalae said as she chuckled devilishly on the inside to herself.

"Shalae! What did you do? Why would you go and get Brian angry! Why are you starting trouble?"

"Momma! I'm not the one starting the trouble! I'm sick of fixing my face with all kinds of makeup before I head into work. My boss knows and so do the people I work with. I'm tired of making up excuses. I don't even like makeup!"

"But Shalae, you know Brian will come after you. Just like your father did with me. It's not worth it baby, it's not! Why don't you go see that nice lady that you've been talking to lately, what is her name? Mrs. C. something?"

"Momma, please let me do this. I will be just fine. After today, Brian will no longer test me, mark my words he won't. Listen, I have to head into work. I will call you when I get out. Plus, Ms. C. doesn't see me until Friday after work. She is helping momma, she is. I'll talk to you later, love you."

As Shalae approached work, she was excited yet terrified to walk through the doors...

Chapter 6
Shalae's escape

Shalae walked into work, and couldn't help but notice everyone staring at her. It was as though they saw a ghost. She walked as fast as she could to the elevator, and to her luck no one got on with her. She had no idea what that was all about but it was creepy. Shalae worked in a big communications building and had to go to the 4th floor to get to her office.

She sold medical instruments to Hospitals, Doctors, Medical Colleges, Universities and some Research centers. Shalae loved her job and some of the people she worked with. They were like her fairy tale family that she always dreamed of. But today seemed like she was stepping into guarded territory...

"Hey Shalae girl, how are you doing?" Yvette was always so giddy in the morning.

"Yvette, I could ask you the same thing. What's going on around here? I walked into the lobby downstairs and everyone was staring at me. What is going on, did I miss something?" Yvette just stood up and gave Shalae her makeup mirror from her desk.

"Yea girl, you forgot to put on your shades this morning. You know makeup can't hide what Brian did to you. Girl, when are you going to leave him?" Yvette asked.

"You mean that's why everyone was staring at me?" Shalae had this pretend dumb look on her face as if she didn't know that was the reason, but deep down she knew.

"Girl, have you seen your face! Look at it in the mirror. He jacked you up good this time I see. What was the reason this time? You didn't move fast enough up the stairs or something? Girl, I don't know how you can still live with him."

"I love him Yvette! I mean it's not as bad as it seems. Brian is really a good person. But I'm working on leaving him; I just need a little more time. I do believe after today he won't be hitting me ever again." Shalae shouted at Yvette without really raising her voice so the office couldn't hear their conversation.

"Shalae! That man doesn't love you. But his fist sure loves the hell out of your face! I mean c'mon, you yourself said you watched your mother go through hell at the hands of your own father, so why would you put yourself in that position? Have you even told Brian about the baby yet? What if he hurts you so bad you lose the baby? Have you thought about that?" Yvette said as she folded her arms in anger and turned her chair around.

Yvette was coming on strong, but Shalae knew it was because she cared about her and the baby. She didn't want to see anything happen to Shalae. But what she didn't know was Shalae had really planned on leaving Brian, just as soon as she saved up enough money to be okay. Shalae was stashing a few dollars away in a shoe box and as well as a separate safe that he had no idea about. A tip that Ms. C told her to do for herself just in case she did decide leave, because with money in bank accounts he would find her.

"Yvette, I am going to tell him about the baby tonight over dinner. Let me borrow some of your foundation, I left mine at home."

"Shalae, nothing is gonna help that black and blue eye of yours, you need to find some shades to put on. You know you have to meet with the new supervisor today about your position. How are going to meet her with that eye? I will go find you some."

Yvette was right, Shalae needed to leave him, but she needed to get a little revenge before she did that. Her plan was all set too. Nothing was going to stop her this time. Yvette finally made it back with some shades for her to put on.

Shalae looked at Yvette with one eyebrow lifted and said, "Girl, who do these shades belong too?"

With her mouth twisted to the side and eyes rolling Yvette said, "Does it matter? They look like reading glasses so just put them on your face! At least you will look professional when you go talk to the big lady. Are you excited? I am so happy for you girl! This is just what you needed to get a fresh start. So let's cover up that eye."

"Yvette you know how I feel about makeup. I don't need it." Against her own decision, Shalae took the makeup.

"Girl, if you don't fix that eye of yours, you'll need a new job. Now fix your face because Miss Peterson is coming."

As Yvette applied the MAC foundation, Shalae stood up to check herself in the big mirror from her desk. That's when she saw the Big Boss

Lady walking down the hallway coming to get her for the hiring interview. This interview was to make sure she still wanted the position, which was a supervisory position, as well as sign some paperwork, and get her financial forms in order. New position meant new money, which could result in a new location.

"Shalae Smith, my name is Miss Peterson and I am your hiring interviewer. Are you ready to step your game up?"

"Yes I am!"

"Glad to hear it. Follow me Shalae." Miss Peterson said as she started to head down the hallway to the conference room.

"Good luck girl!" Yvette whispered to her as Shalae left the cubicle with a pen and notepad and followed Miss Peterson to the end of the hallway of the office. Shalae was on her way to a new beginning and was very excited. The whole hiring process took about 2 hours. There was a lot of paperwork to fill out, videos to watch and hands to shake. Just as Shalae was about to shake the VP's hand, Miss Peterson came over to her very nervously.

Miss Peterson gently grabbed Shalae by her hand and pulled her off to the side from the meeting. "Shalae, you have an emergency call at the front desk. You can take it over in that office in the corner to give you some privacy."

"Thank you Miss Peterson."

"Oh, call me Janice, your one of us now. I hope everything is alright. Keep me posted. Just walk through those brown doors and turn left."

"Thanks Janice and I will. I'm sure everything is alright."

As Shalae headed through the double brown doors, her heart started to beat faster and faster, because she knew she would be getting a call. Shalae knew it would be Brian crying like a little bitch! He wouldn't have the nerve to call the police after all the things she knew about him. But Shalae wanted her revenge and this would be it. She saw the phone off the hook but her body was trembling to pick it up. She was really afraid of what was at the end of the line. Would it be Brian or the police? Only one way to find out… Shalae picked up the line….

"Shalae Smith?"

"Yes this is Shalae Smith and who is this?"

The voice on the other line sounded concerned yet calm; almost nurturing. "This is Nurse Meadows over at the County Hospital. There is a young man named Brian that was brought in by the ambulance and says you're his wife. Are you his wife?"

"No, but go on…" Shalae really wasn't interested in what the nurse had to say. She was tired of the beatings.

"Well somehow he has swallowed several pieces of glass and he is in critical condition. Would you happen to know who did this to him?"

"Yea, maybe… Is he going to live?" Shalae questioned because she wanted to be sure of the validity of the Nurse's concerned tone. She didn't think she left that much in the sauce.

"Well yes, he will recover, but he won't be able to speak. Can you come down here? He really needs to have someone here with him."

"Yea I guess when I'm done I will try to make it. But don't count on it. I will see what I can do." Shalae could tell the nurse was as shocked at her response as Shalae was. But this made Shalae feel powerful and safe.

As Shalae went back to the meeting Janice approached her with yet another issue. This time, her power would be taken out of her just like that…

"Shalae, I don't know how to say this, but the police are here to see you. Does this have something to do with that phone call?"

"Janice, I hope not. Let me go find out what they want. I will be right back. Don't worry everything is okay."

As the policemen were walking down the hallway, Shalae started to walk towards them signaling that she was the Shalae they were looking for. But when they finally reached her, she was not prepared for the news they gave her at all…

Antoinette Lakey

Born & raised in San Antonio, Texas, Antoinette Lakey desired to enter the world of nursing. Through her struggles with childhood abuse she needed to find a way to escape the demons that plagued her life. At the early age of 11 her outlet was simply journaling and that is what saved her life. Growing up she believed that abuse was normal and there was no safety net. She was "discovered" by her high school English teacher and was told, "Write baby girl, it will make you whole." Writing is what she did. Nursing & Social services were her passion and she learned to take her demons of sexual, physical & verbal abuse and use them in a positive manner instead of a crutch. She utilized her love for writing and taking care of others and encompassed it all in the social services field.

Ms. Lakey was first published last summer in the Delphine Publications Anthology, "Between the Sheets", as well as an up and coming columnist with AAMBC. She is presently inking her way into Naughty Ink Press' Anthology,"Untapped: Collection of Erotic Firsts" to be released in the Fall. Ms. Lakey is known in the world of Erotica as "JusMe". She is presently is penning her first novel which deals with domestic abuse.

Ms. Lakey is the mother of two and grandmother of one. She presently works in the Social Services field and finds that the best ways to reach those that many believe are unreachable.

WHY I WROTE:

After many years of physical & mental abuse, on May 31, 2001, my Aunt Juanita Reid broke. Her estranged husband of 20+ years arrived to their home and announced that he was in love with someone else and wanted a divorce. Aunt Nita murdered him, her 11 year old daughter and after a 14 hour standoff killed herself. Her sole sibling Deborah believes that the idea that he would treat her the way he did and then leave her was unbearable. She took her daughter with her to avoid undue burden on remaining family members. As a survivor of physical, sexual & mental abuse, Antoinette believes that it is imperative for others to know that the words sting and leave scars that are far worse than the physical. They go away, the emotional is there forever.

LINKS:
WWW.AUTHORJUSME.COM
Iam4utnv@ymail.com
ladyfelicia@authorjusme.com
Facebook: http://www.facebook.com/author.jusme

"Bitch, don't you ever tell me No, again, you don't have that right. You my woman! Don't you ever think that you will belong to anyone else, do you understand?"

The first time that she remembers Treys' hand across her face it was because she told him she was tired when he demanded sex. She had been at the office since six a.m., it was half past 8, she had been in a deposition that had taken over four hours, and they did not have lunch. He called her in the car on the way home, they talked like normal, and he told her that he had a long day as well. Trey as an architect worked long tedious hours in his firm. They would never dare to compare their stress levels because they each knew they were different. He loved his job just as much as she did hers. Being the City attorney was difficult enough without ridiculing and downplaying our work.

When she arrived home, Trey had ordered take out and picked it up, he was always thoughtful, He figured they were both tired why stress. They ate their dinner together, watched CNN, and discussed the upcoming City Council election.

"Honey, I've had a really long day, I think I'm going to turn in,"

She leaned over and kissed Trey softly on the lips he was so thoughtful and so loving, but all she could think of was taking a long hot shower and climbing in bed and drifting off to sleep. They had a long weekend planned and her parents had invited them to come over after church on Sunday. They had not had dinner with them in a while and Syrai's Dad said that he missed his baby girl. "

"Hey baby its' cool I understand, my hotshot sexy wife has court tomorrow, I gotcha boo!" ooh how she loved that man.

She proceeded to jump in the shower. She must have been in the shower for a minute because she remembers Trey coming in and mentioning that if he heard Lyfe Jennings one more time, he was going to scream. She laughed and he just continued mumbling under his breath, he then just stood there and watched, she became somewhat oblivious to him and I continued to sing and dance in the shower. She got out oiled up her body and massaged pertinent parts. She decided that since she was definitely going to bed, she put on my old t-shirt and her thong. Wrapped her hair turned off the stereo and climbed into the bed, cuddled up to her pillow, and quickly dozed off to sleep. She noticed Trey came to bed around 3 a.m. and jumped in the shower, he climbed into bed and they spooned for about half an hour. Trey was not going to sleep, and under most circumstances, she never turn down her husband because he does so much and she loved him to the end, but tonight she was just exhausted. "Trey, honey lets' do this in the morning let's get some rest, please" as she turned to Trey to utter these words, that's when she I realized that she smelled Hennessey. Trey tended to drink when he 'stressed. "Baby I need you I need my wife, my beautiful sexy wife, I need to feel you baby." Trey wasn't letting up he kept saying that he just needed to relax. She slowly pulled away from him and realized he was gripping her arm tighter than she thought he was. "Trey honey, you're hurting me, please let me go!"Syrai was thinking he did not realize how hard he was squeezing her arm. Trey mumbled something that she could not understand, and let go of his death grip... She rolled out of the bed slowly, as to not agitate him. She stood up, Treys' eyes were glazed over, and she realized he was a little more than drunk and she did not like the look in his eyes and she told him so. She turned walked to the edge of the bed, grabbed her pillow and pulled the comforter off the bed and before she could turn around a walk out Trey was in her face.

"Syrai, I'm going' to ask you one time and one time only, who in the hell are you fuckin?" She was taken a little off guard because she love Trey and she loves him with all of her heart and she would never think of cheating on him. "Baby, what are you talking about?" All the while Trey is in her face backing me up against a wall. "I was at your office the other day and I saw that old motherfucker looking at you." She could not for the life of her think about whom he could have been talking about. Then it dawned on her that he was talking about Mr. Simmons, the new civil litigant. She had only met the man once and there was no love lost between them. He asked questions, she answered. she looked at Trey, and was near tears as she cried out, "No baby I am not sleeping with anyone, I promise you that". Trey was crying at this point and all he kept saying was, "I should've seen this coming."

"What baby, seen what coming? Trey I love you "She felt the sting across her face with his fist...

THE BEGINNING

Trey and Syrai began to date their sophomore year in College and "he" decided that they were going to be exclusive when she told him she wanted to see other people. They had been seeing each other for eight months and she was getting a little bored on the dating scene. She told him either they were going to be together or they are not. He called himself calling her bluff, said, "fine then." They broke up, and she started seeing someone else almost immediately. She was not happy seeing somebody else but hell, Trey decided to be an ass and she was able to walk away. Trey waited two weeks and let her play the field, then decided he wanted his girl back. "Baby no one could ever love you like I can" and he kissed her as she has never been kissed. The next three years were relatively uneventful and sure, there were minor altercations. Trey would sometimes accidentally push her into a wall or there was one point where she yelled at him. He said he was in another world with his kid's football training camp that he coached and I startled him. He jumped and accidentally backhanded her. Nevertheless, she realized now it was her fault and she should never force him to be angry with her.

It would still take Syrai years to realize that Treys' abuse was a pattern, a very ugly pattern; there were many occasions where Trey would have an accidental meeting of his fist with Syrai's face and body. He was very careful not to leave a bruise. That wasn't acceptable. Trey felt like he wasn't abusing his wife; he was teaching her how to be a "proper" wife.

Syrai had graduated from Law School on Saturday and her parents were ecstatic. Her parents gave her a brand new Camry and Daddy informed her that he had paid cash and all she had to pay was insurance. "Anything for my baby girl," Daddy was so proud of her and Mom just kept smiling and telling her that this was a new beginning for her. Her brother Joseph kept telling her how proud he was, but something about how he said it just was not right. "Syrai, I just need you to promise me to reconsider. You can do better than this chump you hooked up with. He's no good for you I know this and you need to know." "Joseph, I'm ok I'm not going to do anything I wouldn't want to do you know me better than that, I love him but I'm not stupid". She tried to reassure her older brother but he just did not appear to hear her.

He hugged her and told her if she ever needed anything, he has her back. She tried desperately to ignore what he was saying but Syrai kept hearing him tell her that Trey was no good for her. She shrugged it off and went right back into Treys' arms. From that day forward, there was no love lost between Trey and Joseph.

When Trey proposed to me it was beautiful. My parents had a surprise party for me to celebrate my graduation. Before the end of the night right after my Grandparents gave me a roundtrip ticket to Spain, Trey got down on one knee in front of everyone, "Syrai, you have been the love of my life since high school and I would be a fool to lose you. I have lost you once and I will never do it again, you are my heart girl. I want to spend the rest of my life with you. Syrai Davis will you marry me?" I was shocked and I just stood there trying to hold back tears. My best friend Tamara walked over hit me on my shoulder, "Uh, can you say yes fool! The man is on his knees." I looked at Trey and then my parents and I replied, "Yes. Trey I would love to become your wife." I very carefully avoided looking in the direction of Joseph. We were wed 1 year later with enough time to plan the wedding of the century. Six on each side of our bridal party it was fabulous. "I am officially Mrs. Trey Jackson, ooh that sounds good."

Dilemma

Trey and Syrai had been married 6 years and chose to wait until their careers were established. They had bought a home and wanted to be ready to share their lives before having children. It was a decision that they did not tread on lightly as they both came from troubled childhoods. Even though she and Trey and tended to slip up every now and then she was somewhat shocked when she went in for her yearly check-up and my doctor informed me that she was 3 ½ months pregnant. How could she possibly tell Trey?

"Syrai, this was not part of the plan. We were supposed to wait. How could you do this to me? How could you do this to us?" I was ashamed that I had done this to us. I did not do it on purpose, I really didn't, however maybe subconsciously this is what I wanted. Nevertheless, I did not want to betray my husband. Trey was even angrier when he researched and found out it was too late for an abortion. Trey and I discussed how we would handle it and decided there was really nothing we could do but just deal with it. Trey said that he was okay. He thought about it and was okay with the idea that I was going to give him a son. At the five month mark Trey was enthused that this was sonogram week. He told all of his staff this was the day that he would name his son. Trey had an ongoing bet with me that my baby bump was so big because it was his son. I kept telling him it was his beautiful daughter that I was carrying. He didn't find that quite as amusing as I. He just continuously glared at me, never touching me, but it had me worried none the less.

We arrived at the obstetrician's office excited. Trey decided that he was going to stand at the end of the table and watch the nurse as she gelled up my belly. "I need to get a good look at my boy Sarai." The nurse smiled and took her time. She asked me what I wanted. I responded, "Just a healthy baby…" She laughed and said, "Well one of you isn't going to be too pleased." Trey chuckled and said, "See Sarai, I told you that was my boy." He walked over to the nurse and raised his fist for a fist bump. "Uh Mr. Davis, you should say hello to your little girl."

"No, I think you're wrong, look again."

"Sir, her legs are open there's nothing resembling a penis there. Its' a girl."

Trey glared at me like he never had before. "Sarai fix it! This is supposed to be a happy time for us; you are supposed to have my son. That would make me happy." Trey shook his head and walked out. I walked out of the doctor's office and went into the foyer and realized Trey was not there. I walked down to the lobby expecting to see Trey sitting in his Mercedes. He was not there. I looked into the parking spot where we parked and his car was gone. I located my phone in my purse. "Trey honey, where are you?"

"I'm on 1604. I need to think Sarai. This was not the plan"

"Baby what you are saying?"

"Damn it Sarai! Its' bad enough I wasn't ready for no damn baby and now we find out your ass can't even give me a son? I gotta think Sarai."

I began to sob, "Trey, are you leaving me?" The phone line went dead; he had to lose his signal. I called a cab. I arrived home to find that Trey had packed a vast majority of his clothes, but I began to look for a note. I searched high and low only to find nothing. Trey was gone for 3 ½ weeks. He arrived home just as I was beginning to think he didn't care. That made me realize he had come to his senses.

I worked diligently though the morning and my client I had a deposition with this afternoon was driving me crazy. The case I was working on was a nasty high profile divorce and there was a lot of property. I hope we can get some headway today. My secretary Janise chimed in as she was preparing to leave. "Mrs. Jackson, your husband is one line one." "Thank you Jesus, Trey honey, where are you?" Hey baby, we need to talk. I just needed some time to think about some things." I was so ecstatic. He has finally come to his senses. "Okay boo, I'll meet you at home around seven. I know you're working late." That works honey, I'll see you tonight." Then we disconnected.

I decided I was going to run by Fischers, pick up a few things, and cook Trey a nice dinner. We needed to celebrate. I just kept reminding myself that Trey came to his senses and was now happy about his little girl. I decide to cook Treys' favorite meal; meatloaf, mashed potatoes and green beans. I made tea for myself and had white wine for Trey.

Trey walked in with Chinese takeout and didn't look too happy that I had cooked dinner. "Hey baby, it's alright. We just have lunch for work tomorrow." Trey grabbed me and kissed me so gently that it made me weak in the knees. I pulled back a little and looked him in the eyes. "Baby I'm so happy you're home. I missed you last night. You know this house is cold and lonely at night." Trey looked me in the eyes as well and said, "I'm sorry baby. I'll never do it again." That's' my Trey! Oh how I love my man.

Dinner went well, so well in fact that there was very little meatloaf left. I quickly cleaned up the kitchen. Trey watched the news and everything was just as it needed to be peaceful.

I showered and put on something sexy for Trey when he came to bed. We still had not talked about whatever it was that he wanted to discuss. Trey came to bed around midnight and climbed into bed next to me. He held me close and entered me from behind. He felt so good and I realized just how much I loved him. He turned me over, kissed my lips, "Syrai, I love you baby. Always remember that." Trey slowly reached down and as he was on top of me he kissed my breast one by one as he massaged my clit. "Oh baby you feel so good! You are so wet. Trey I love you and will take care of you always." Trey then entered me and made love to me until the wee hours of the morning. We both decided that we would call our offices and say we would be in a little late. We then lie in bed. I lay my head on Treys chest and said nothing as I massaged his manhood to erection. "You like that baby?" You know I do Sara. Take care of Daddy... I slid down and placed his erect cock into my mouth. "Yeah baby, let me show you just how much I love you." I rose after sucking him to near climax, as I was afraid the semen would make me sick. I arose and climbed on top of him. "Baby, I love you forever." I wanted Trey to know that I loved him as equally as he loved me. He felt so good and I grinded him until we both climaxed. I was always told that when you came together it was a sign of unity and I wanted us to be as close as possible. We fell asleep and awoke at noon. "Oh shit Trey! It's late! We need to get up." I tried to jump up and Trey pulled me back down on the bed." "Hold on, baby I called your office about an hour ago. You were sleeping so well. I called and told them you were a little under the weather." "Trey you just take care of me so well." It's only because I love you sleeping beauty." "I love you too baby." As I got ready to grab my husband and kiss him he pulled away. "C'mon baby, why don't you get up and lets go to IHOP for breakfast. "IHOP? Baby you hate IHOP." "Anything for my girl..." "Okay, I'll go shower and get ready. It's not often you take me somewhere you dislike." I quickly got up and showered. I put on one of my revealing tops that Trey liked so much and a pair of jeans. I was not quite as big as I thought and was happy that I could still wear my jeans. Trey always said he liked how the jeans cupped my ass and raised it up just right. I was happy and all I could think of was continuing to please my husband. I always want to let him know how much I love him. I walked out of the bedroom and called Treys' name, "Trey honey, where are you?" "I am in the nursery baby. I will be right down." Syrai paused and peeked around the corner. Trey was sitting on the twin bed in the nursery holding a teddy bear.

"Syrai, baby let's talk before we leave for breakfast. Come sit."

"Ok honey, sure."

"Syrai, there is nothing more than I can say except that I love you and if the baby was a boy things could be so much different."

"Trey, what are you saying?"

Trey grabbed her, and kissed her deeply, tears welling up in his eyes. "Syrai, I love you baby."

"I love you too honey, I always will."

Syrai was not aware that Trey had hidden a .45 caliber revolver under the pillow behind her. Trey slowly but swiftly raised the revolver to Syrais' head and shot her once in the temple. Syrai immediately had a blank stare and closed her eyes. She wasn't dead.

Trey called his father-in-law and asked him to come to the house. He told him that Syrai was not feeling well and he was concerned. Syrais' Dad would never come alone. He always asked Joseph to accompany him just in case he needed to convince Syrai to get medical attention. Joseph rang the doorbell and immediately heard a single gunshot. The door was not locked. He immediately ran inside the house to find Trey dead in the hallway outside of the nursery with a single gunshot to his head. Syrai was positioned on the bed and she was still breathing. Syrai remained on life support for 45 days until it was safe to deliver the baby. The family believed that Syrai would've wanted it that way.

THE END

Danielle "Dani" Taylor

Here is a little about myself. My name is Danielle Taylor. I'm married to a wonderful man, Rodney Taylor, and am the mother of 3 teenage children. I am a sister, friend and the editor of So Fyh Magazine Online. I'm also an aspiring author. There were a few points in my life when I felt like I was alone. Then I found out that God has always been with me through all my ups and downs. No matter what life threw me, He was there. I seem to have come out a better person in spite of it all.

Looking back, there have been some important people in my life, who saw me through some tough moments. God is my strength and the source of my being. He has granted me the love of my children. If it had not been for the love of my children I don't know where I would be. God and the man that He placed into my life have been my rock. My husband is my soul-mate. He was made for me. I have seen so much and he has helped me through a lot of it.

WHY I WROTE:

I am proud to be able to contribute to this anthology and assist in helping women, children and men who struggle daily with the fears of not knowing when the one they love will hurt them again.

LINKS:
www.leestylezsofyhphotography.com
www.iamdanidiva.com
www.sofyhmagazineonline.com
www.mydivathoughts.blogspot.com
www.sofyhbookreviews.com

Voices Behind the Tears

Dear Diary,

Today wasn't like any other day
Will this pain go away
As I glance into the mirror I don't know
the person that is looking back at me
With all the bruises and marks
Why am I hiding my face in the dark
Isolated from my family and some of my friends
But today I believe he hates me and maybe he really
loves me in the end
Makeup covers only so much
My soul and body hurts form the slightest touch
I have been with my boyfriend for over 3 years
which you already know
Wow where did all the time go

He was nice and sweet at first
My friends' tell me all the time I need
to leave before I end up in a hearse
I'm always doing something wrong from the way I wear my hair,
or even say his name.
I don't understand why I feel so ashamed,
I try to be the best girlfriend that a guy could ever have.
When I tell him I love him he just looks at me and laughs
My heart loves him so much
Today his love came through with a right punch
I can't leave because he needs me

I understand that he tells me he's sorry for all he's done
Yesterday he threatened me with his gun
I know that I must get away from him
Or one day I may lose my life
I can't help and dream of the day he said he'll make me his wife

I know that I'm dreaming of is a fairytale that will never happen
Sitting here in my room, wondering should
I just pack my bags and leave for good

Saving Lives Through Lit

His charming ways, his smile makes my heart melt
Silly me I fall for it all the time
One of these days he's going to love me to death
That is what he always tells me I love you to death

Tonight I pray that I can make it through another day
Until I write again thanks Diary for listening
If I never write again, my boyfriend loved me to death
I fought the best way I knew how.

Love,

Troubled Hearted

Earnestine Moore

Ernestine Moore was born in 1965 in Cleveland, Ohio to Essie Moore and Harold Brook, whom she never met. Brook died before she was born but she considers her real father who she loves with all her heart to be Samuel Williams. Moore has been a resident of Detroit since she was two. She became a teen mother at the age of fifteen, dropping out of school and only receiving a seventh grade education. At the age of twenty-three, she already had six children and a daughter that she did not give birth to. Now, she is a grandmother of twelve beautiful kids and lives on the east side of Detroit with a disability caused by an accident while working on a transportation job. This is the first part of her book, which she considers a great fulfillment of her life. She is currently working on the second part of her autobiography.

LINKS:
www.ernestinemoore.com
www.facebook.com/ernestine.moore1

IN THE LIFE AND MIND OF A PHYSICAL, MENTALLY, SEXUALLY & VERBALLY ABUSED WOMAN*
by Ernestine Moore

THIS IS MY SURVIVING STORY

Except from Chapters 5 and 6...

A portion of the proceeds from the Novel upon release will be donated to Saving Lives Through Lit.

Path of Destruction

I went to dramatic measures to destroy myself because of all the physical and mental abuse. Deep down in my soul I was suffering.

Lena was living with us again, separated from Jo-Jo. I wasn't too thrilled about the situation because of the violent history between us. I also didn't understand why she continually whipped her older son with an electric extension cord for inexcusable reasons. She beat him for wetting the bed instead of seeking medical treatment. It was obvious he had a problem, and I thought it was hypocritical for her to whip him when she had the same problem growing up, even through her marriage. The abuse she inflicted upon him was very cruel. She'd taken an electric extension cord, wrapped it around his neck three times, and started choking him all because his little brother said he hit him. And he had no one to rescue him. She was not concerned with who she hurt.

My Little cousin slept in the room with my brother, and Lena slept in the living room. One night while I was asleep in the dining room on the floor I was awakened to whispering. I heard a female voice; it was Lena. Then I heard a man whispering. I didn't recognize his voice because he was whispering really low. I lay there quietly listening. He then said something and I recognized the voice. My heart sank. I was outraged. The man was Chicken. Then they started moaning. I instantly started crying. She was having sex with the man that I was infatuated with. I was so angry, hurting inside, and wanted to hurt them. But I couldn't because we had a secret, a forbidden affair because of our age difference.

Promiscuity with preference...

I was angry and mentally destroyed. I started using and abusing my body. I don't know who I was trying to hurt, but I was only hurting myself at the time. I didn't care anymore. No one cared about me, and mentally and physically, I was damaged. I was not able to be satisfied sexually or mentally because of the rapes. I was promiscuous, having sex with men for fun. The guys I was with were very generous, and I was compensated with money after having sex, but I never asked. I didn't always have sex to get money. I never had sex with a lot of guys, just the ones named in this story, and it was never back-to-back. It could be a week or two or months before I had sex. I really didn't like sex. Like I said, it was only to hurt myself.

I'd met this old man name Joe-bob in my neighborhood, and whenever I needed money, I met him in the alley behind his house or at the corner store. People were spreading rumors that I was having sex with him but I wasn't. He was an old man that liked me and would give me money when I asked.

Joe-bob introduced me to a guy named Williams but everyone called him Bill. He had just separated from his wife. Bill wasn't appealing to the eyes, but I didn't care. All I wanted was his money. He was also giving me money without having sex me, but I planned to reward him with sex. He invited me to his house. Once inside, he took me to the living room sat me on the couch. I wanted to see his bedroom, but he wouldn't let me. I didn't care anyway.

My first sexual encounter with Bill was not that good. He per-formed oral sex. I don't know why, but it felt nasty. I didn't enjoy it. The only other time oral sex was performed on me was by my mother's boyfriends, JB and Ray. I believe that was the reason why I didn't like oral sex.

Bill was one of three guys I had sex with within a two-month span. Dennis was another. He lived upstairs from us. He also was the brother of one of my mother's friends. With Dennis, it started out with us just flirting and over time it lead to sex. We would give a signal and meet in the basement to have sex. Our basement was divided and had two small rooms. We met down there three or four times and no one knew we would.

Tommy Bright was the other man I had sex with. He was a childhood friend who lived next door to me when I was seven. I ran into him once while I was on my way to Nancy's house. He was visiting friends in my neighborhood. We talked for a few minutes, and then he asked me for my address so he could stop by some time.

A day or two later he did. After we talked about what was going on in each other's lives. We made plans to be alone. I had him meet me in my garage and we had sex. A week later, we had sex again. That was the last time I saw Tommy Bright. I had sex with Bill on two more occasions.

The following month, March, I was late. I hadn't started my menstrual cycle yet. I was feeling sick, nauseated, and started to wonder if I was pregnant. I kept my suspicion a secret out of fear. I knew for sure the next month. I was really scared. I was fourteen and I was pregnant. I didn't want to tell my mother because I didn't want her to make me have an abortion.

The first person I told was Williams because he was the last man I'd had sex with, so I assumed he was the father. He told me that he would help me take care of the baby. All I could do was take him at his word. Now that I knew that I was pregnant I really wasn't going to go to school. I didn't want to take a risk of being injured just in a fight. I would leave the house as usual; make a detour to sneak back into my favorite place to hide, my basement.

When I was in the basement I could hear everything Mama was doing. I would wait and watch her leave to go to the doctor, and then I would sneak upstairs, fix something to eat and sit at the window to watch for when she got back home. Sometimes I would almost get caught because she would come from a different direction. I had to run, turn off the TV, and run real fast to the basement. When I skipped school I would have to wait until I got home to eat because I didn't have any money. Now that I was pregnant, I had to eat.

Amy told me that she didn't want to go to school. I hadn't let anyone know about my skipping school. I trusted her, so I let her in on my little secret. In the morning, we left for school, made a quick detour, walked down the alley and through the unlocked window to our basement. We hid in the small room in the back. We listened out for Mama to leave. I was showing her everything I did just in case she wanted to skip again. When Mama left, we went upstairs. I told her I would sneak some food, watch TV, and sit by the window, watching out for Mama. When we saw her coming we would run back to the basement. And when we knew school was about to let out, we climbed out the window, walked halfway to school, turned around, and walked back home.

My sister and her friends discovered my hiding place, which I was unaware of until later. Early one morning before I left home to go to a friend's house, Amy told me that she and her friend decided that they didn't want to go to school. She repeated the routine I'd showed her, listening out to hear Mama and Lena leave. We never knew how long they would be gone and had to watch out.

While hiding in the basement, they decided to smoke. When they were finished, instead of throwing the cigarette butt in the drain or sink, my sister threw it out the window. It landed right in front of Mama and Lena. Amy and her friend were caught. From that day on, Mama or Lena would check to see if the basement window was locked before they left, but that didn't stop me.

I came up with another way to get in and hide. They never knew. Before I would leave the house, I would go in the basement, go to the neighbor's side of the basement and unlock their window or unlock their back door and hide on our side. And when I heard Mama or Lena walk into the kitchen to come down the basement to make sure the window was locked, I would run back on the neighbor's side and hide in the back room. I'd make sure I was real quiet, my heart beating real fast, thinking I was going to get caught when they were in the basement a long time.

When I heard them going back up the stairs and out the door, I waited a minute just to make sure they didn't come back in the house. Then I'd sneak upstairs, get something to eat, and not taking any risks, I went back in the basement to wait until it was time to leave. I laugh now when I think about what I had to do to not be caught. I had to stop when it became hard for me to fit through the window.

It was hot outside, and school was about to let out for summer vacation. I just went and hid out at the park, not eating until I came home from the school I wasn't attending. I was getting bigger and had to change my appearance so I started wearing big clothes to cover up.

Summer arrived and I didn't want to draw attention to myself. It was hot outside and I was supposed to be wearing summer clothes, but instead I wore a big tee shirt. I knew eventually I would have to tell somebody, and the only person I trusted was Lady H. I went to her house and told her. She asked me what I was going to do. I said I wanted my baby. I was already four months. She asked if I was going to tell my mother. I told her not yet. She asked if I wanted her to tell my mother. I said no, not yet. I knew I had to soon, so I waited until I was five months.

I figured I was safe, that my mother couldn't make me have an abortion at five months. When I was at Lady H's house, she asked me again, if I wanted her to tell my mother. This time, I said yes. I knew I hadn't seen a doctor, and I hadn't been taking care of myself right. As we walked to my house, I saw Mama wasn't as high as she usually was. I was nervous and scared.

Lady H sat down next to mama on the couch in our dining room. I stood up real nervous as she started to tell her. At first, my mother didn't say anything, and didn't have any reaction to the news. She waited until Lady H left. My mother walked up to me, didn't say anything, and just went wild. Without any regard to my condition, she started beating me. I looked at her in disbelief. She pushed me down on the bed and just started hitting and punching me all my face, and chest. Then she sat on my stomach and continued to beat me. She started calling me every cuss word she could think of. I felt she was trying to kill my baby. She was hitting me like she was a wild animal just like all the other times.

I felt I had to defend myself. I snapped, and I started fighting back. My mother was trying to kill me or my baby, and I had to stop her. I somehow freed myself. I got up and ran out the house, she ran right behind me, telling me to come back here. I was running, screaming and crying. Our neighbor, Diana came running out her door to see what was going on. When I saw her, I started running toward her for safety. Before I got to the steps, I felt pain in my back. My mother had thrown a brick at me, and it hit me in middle of my back. With Diana's help, I got up the stairs to her porch, and into her house, with Mama trying to get in. Diana stopped her and told her she wasn't getting in to hit me, and I wasn't coming out until she calmed down. Mama left off her porch, cussing, saying what she going to do to me when I came out.

Diana walked over to me. I was crying, in pain, and disbelief that Mama did this to me while I was pregnant. Diana asked me what was going on. I told her that Mama just found out I was pregnant and that she just started beating me. Diana made me stay at her house overnight. We talked… I cried as I let loose some of my feelings to her. I let her know some of the things that were going on at my house…

Laura Johnson

Laura Johnson is a first time author with her new novel titled "Where Would I Be". She resides in Memphis, Tennessee, where she attends college and is pursuing her Bachelor's degree in Psychology and Social & Criminal Justice with a minor in forensics. Laura was first bitten by the writing bug three years ago. While writing a journal she began to realize that her story could possibly help others who were going through the same thing.

In 2006, Laura was the victim of an abusive relationship that lasted for two and half years. The relationship was volatile from the beginning. While in this relationship, Laura contemplated suicide almost on a daily basis. If asked, she would immediately tell you that what kept from going through with suicide were her mother and younger brother. "I couldn't leave them with that much pain, no matter what I was going through."

By 2008, Laura had suffered many things at the hand of her abuser. Everything from verbal abuse to rape and she soon decided that she had to get out of the relationship before it was too late. Her last interaction with her abuser consisted of an argument and a fight, which lead to him being arrested. That day he promised he would get even.

In 2009, Laura began to write. She thought that, as her mother had told many times before, that she was not the only woman who had or will ever go through something like this. And this novel is the final product.

WHY I WROTE:

I wanted to participate in this anthology because I want to do my part to bring attention to abuse. Being a domestic violence survivor myself, telling my story may help others who are going through the same thing. The reason I write is because it allows me to share my life, my pain, my success, and my strength to any and every one that reads my book.

LINKS:
Blog: http://laurajohnsonauthor.blogspot.com/
Facebook Fan Page:
http://www.facebook.com/home.php#!/AuthorLauraTJohnson
Twitter: http://twitter.com/#!/authorlauraj

Excerpt from Where Would I Be

Lisa and Carol were finally closing up shop. Lisa packed her briefcase with the remainder of her files and headed home. Getting off the elevator, Lisa said, "I am going to try to get through as many of these as I possibly can. What are you gonna do tonight?"

"I am going to stay in bed with my husband all night."

"Lucky you."

"It could be the same for you someday if you would just let me hook you up. I know…"

"No, Carol."

"He's intelligent, good looking, and has never been married. He's Charles's partner."

"No, Carol. Now go home and have fun."

"Okay. But, don't say I didn't try."

After giving each other a hug, they got in their cars and drove out of the garage in different directions. When Lisa got home, she dropped her things on her couch, looked through her mail, and checked her messages. Going through her mail, Lisa saw that she only had junk mail and her new Avon catalog arrived, which she was happy about because she needed to order some more skin cream and makeup; especially her Oatmeal Body Lotion. She was down to half a bottle. Just thinking about it, she knew it would be a big order this month.

Taking her briefcase and purse upstairs with her, she stopped in one of her guest bedrooms. It was also a home office. She left her briefcase and a stack of bills she was planning to pay tonight on the desk. She then headed to her bedroom to get out of her clothes and do her nightly ritual before getting to work.

After an hour of rejuvenating herself, she headed downstairs to see what she could make a quick dinner out of. Opening her refrigerator, she could already tell her mother had been there. There were two new Tupperware dishes in her refrigerator. Opening them, she found lasagna in one and French bread in the other. "Thank you mommy."

Heading back upstairs to her office with a plate and a glass of white wine, she heard her phone ring. Pushing the speaker button, she said, "Hello?"

"Where the hell have you been?" her friend Nic said, without preamble.

"Working."

"Mm-hmm, I'm walking in."

"I'm upstairs in the office." Lisa then hung up, and started to eat as she booted up her computer.

Her friend walked into the room, and said, "I should shoot you."

"What did I do?"

"You haven't called or stopped by. The only way I knew you were alright was through Pat or Carol. So, I had to come find you myself."

"That's what makes you a great detective."

Nic and Lisa had been friends for the past eleven years. Lisa considered all of her girlfriends to be her sisters, but Nic would always be the one she was a closest too. How could she not, Nic saved her life.

"So, what brings you out this way?" Lisa asked her.

"No first things first anymore?" Nic asked, referring to Lisa's plate.

"My mother has been here, so you know there is…"

"I'll be right back," Nic said, as she left the room.

A couple of minutes later, she was back with a plate of her own and a glass of wine herself. "So, what are you doing?"

"Leftover work that me and Carol didn't finish today. You had to work tonight?"

"Just got off." Nic was a detective for the ninth precinct. Make that a great detective, at least that's what Lisa thought.

"Anything strange or exciting happen today?"

"No, but something in the area of déjà vu happened."

"What?" Lisa asked, as she continued to eat before getting to work.

"Well, John and I got a call for domestic violence."

"Why, were you—" Then Lisa figured it out. "Oh. The wife or girlfriend?"

"The wife. The husband said she just kept pushing him. He couldn't control himself."

"How did he…do it?" Lisa asked.

"He beat her to death," Nic said in a sad voice.

"How bad?"

"If it wasn't for the pictures in the house, we would have never recognized her."

"My God. What will happen to him?"

"He will be charged. For what? That depends on the DA."

"Wow."

"Yeah, I know."

For the rest of the night, Lisa and Nic talked while Lisa finished up her work. By midnight, Nic was gone and Lisa was in bed.

The next morning, Lisa made it to work by eight-thirty and was ready for work.

"Good morning," Carol sang, when she walked in at nine on the dot.

"Good morning, to you. I see your night went well."

"My night went great," Carol said with a big smile on her face.

"I would ask what you two did last night, but I'm sure I'm too young to hear those sorts of things."

"Yes, I don't want to corrupt your little mind. So, did you get any work done?"

"Yeah, I got the majority of them done. But I still have a lot to do."

"Well, give me half and I'll get started on those. And don't worry about any meetings today; you have a clear day to do some catch up."

Lisa handed her six files, then said, "Bless you. Oh, wait one of those are from Marc. I have to work that one."

"Buzz me if you need," Carol said, as she walked out of the office.

Lisa worked through the day, until Carol buzzed her to let her know she was leaving for lunch. Lisa continued to work on the accounts for the rest of the day. She actually worked through lunch. When she looked up, Carol was walking in with her coat and purse. "It's quitting time, lady."

Lisa looked up from her computer screen, and said, "I know. This day has truly gotten away from me. I didn't even get to eat lunch."

"I know. That's why I am bringing over takeout and you pro-vide the wine."

"I don't know, Carol, I just wanted to go home and soak in my tub."

"Oh, I'm sorry; you really thought I was asking. No Honey, I'll be at your house by seven-thirty."

"Alright." Lisa was actually glad Carol insisted to come over. She really didn't want to be at home alone tonight with her thoughts of James.

Lisa and Carol split up from each other to get in their cars. Due to it being summer, it was still light out. On the way home, Lisa stopped at the store to pick up two bottles of her favorite Pinot Grigio.

When she got home, she checked her messages. Her mother and Nic left messages. So, she called her mother first.

"Hey, mama."

"Hey."

"What are you up to?"

"Nothing, right now. What about you?"

"Just got home and I'm about to jump in the tub. But, I wanted to give you a call first. Carol is coming over in a little while. She's bringing over some takeout and I have the wine. Why don't you come over and hang out with us?"

"Naw, honey. I'm going to the casino with Marilyn."

"Well, win me some money."

"You already got money, I need that money."

"For what? You need anything?"

"No, baby. I'm fine. Just going for fun."

"Okay, then."

"Ooo, Marilyn just pulled up. I'll talk to you tomorrow."

"Alright. Good luck."

"Thank you. Bye."

After hanging up from her mother, Lisa called Nic.

"Hello," Nic said.

"Hey, what you doing?" Lisa asked.

"Nothing much. What's going on with you?"

"The same. I'm just getting home from work. I'm about to change and get comfortable before Carol gets here."

"How she doing?"

"Fine."

"So, what are you two up to tonight?"

"We're having a gossip fest. Why don't you come over?"

"I don't know, ya'll have room for one more?"

"Girl, please," Lisa said. "Get your butt over here."

"Well, since you put it that way. I'll be over in an hour. Is there anything I can bring?"

"Carol is providing the food. I'm providing the wine, so you can provide the dessert. Call her and tell her to bring enough for you too."

"What is she bringing?" Nic asked.

"You know I didn't ask. Oh well, whatever it is I'll eat it."

"How 'bout I bring some donuts?" Nic laughed.

"Not funny."

"Okay, okay. I'll bring a large cheesecake."

"Perfect! I'll see you in an hour."
"Bye."
"Bye."
When Lisa hung up the phone she looked at her watch and realized she had just enough time for a good soak.

****

Carol and Nic showed up at seven-thirty on the dot. "Hey, ladies. Come on in," Lisa said, as she stepped aside to let them in.

"Thank you," Carol and Nic said in unison.

Lisa led them to the coffee table in the living room where the radio was playing Mary J. Blidge's new CD.

"Alright, ladies, let's get full, in both meanings of the word," Nic said, as they got comfortable in different sections around the table.

Lisa, sitting on the floor up against the big couch, Nic sitting Indian style on the love seat, and Carol sitting on the big couch to the right of Lisa. As the ladies dug into the Chinese food and poured wine, the gossip-fest began.

Carol told them about her next door neighbor who was having an affair. "Two days ago her husband came home early. She must have heard him come in, because the next thing I know, the boyfriend is on the roof buck-naked."

"What?" Nic said, loudly.

"Yes, ma'am. But get this, now he has to quietly put on his clothes while he is still on the roof. Evidently, he wasn't, because the husband comes back outside and looks straight up at the guy. So by now other neighbors and I as well are coming outside to watch the action. All of a sudden the husband comes out of the house and yells at the man, 'You're supposed to clean the pool!' Then he gets the water hose and starts to spray the guy with water. The boyfriend loses his balance and slips and falls off the roof into the woman's flower bush."

By now all of them are in tears from laughing so hard.

"Was he hurt?" Lisa asked.

"No, but then the husband grabs the guy and beats the hell out of him. Charlotte, the wife, calls the police and has them arrest the husband for beating up the boyfriend."

"No, she didn't," Lisa said.

"The hell she didn't," Carol said.

"Is the husband still in jail?" Nic asked.

"Got out the next day, came home while Charlotte was at work and put all her shit out on the curb. I mean every knick knack and bric-a-brac. Then told people that were walking by that they could get whatever they wanted. I got a beautiful vanity set, mirror and all."

"You did not take that woman's vanity set?" Nic said, laughing.

"The hell I didn't. Shit, that's more money in my pocket," Carol said, laughing.

"You better be lucky I'm off duty, Mrs. Carol," Nic said.

"Honey, please, you don't have enough people in your department to arrest everybody in my neighborhood. Hell, those people were fighting over her stuff like it was Christmas Eve. Some of those folks I thought were dead. They probably were and just came back to get free shit."

For the duration of the dinner, all the ladies traded stories until the food was gone and the dessert and wine were on their way to being nonexistent.

Then Carol said, "So, Lisa, are you going to finally tell me who the mystery man is that keep coming by the office?"

"What mystery man?" Nic asked, as she sliced herself another piece of cheesecake.

"That's what I been trying to find out."

"No one. Just someone I used to know. Anybody want any more wine?" Lisa asked, trying to change the subject.

"No! Now come on and tell us who he is," Carol said.

"I know who it is, it's Russell," Nic said.

"No," said Lisa.

Then Nic said, "Jason?"

"Nope."

"Damn, then who?" Carol burst out.

When Lisa didn't say anything or make eye contact with either of them, Nic said, "James?!"

Lisa couldn't even look her friend in the eyes.

"Oh, hell naw!" Nic said, loudly.

As Nic stared at Lisa, Lisa stared at the table, while Carol looked between each lady waiting for one of them to say something.

"What's going on? Don't leave a sista' out," Carol said.

Lisa and Nic looked at Carol and burst out laughing.

"What? I'm a sista' by heart. Now, tell me what's going on?"
"James is Lisa's ex," Nic said, while still looking at Lisa.
"Oh," Carol said, while pouring herself another glass of wine.
Then Nic asked, "What did he want?"
"He said he stopped by to say hello," Lisa said.
"How long did he stay?"
"Not long."
"What did you talk about?"
"Nothing, I told him to leave."
"How many times has he been by the office?"
"Twice. You know, this is starting to feel like an interrogation."
"I'm asking as a friend."
"It doesn't seem like it."
"Look, don't try and change the subject."
"I'm not."
"Yeah, right," Nic said under her breath. Then she said aloud, "Well?"
Lisa sighed and then said, "He just came by to talk."
"About what?"
"He said he had changed and he wanted to apologize."
"Oh, please."
"What does he have to apologize for?" Carol asked.
Neither Lisa nor Nic answered her.
So Carol said, "Hellooo, did I disappear?"
"No, Carol. Why don't you tell her, Lisa?"
The room was completely quiet. It even seemed as if Mary J. Blidge was waiting for an answer.
"We dated about six years ago," Lisa began. "Some things happened and we broke up."
"Like what?" Carol asked.
Lisa didn't answer, so Nic did, "They dated for two years, which a year and a half of those years were spent with him beating her."
"What?" Carol exclaimed.
Lisa still didn't say anything, so Nic continued. "When they first met, according to Lisa, everything was fine. Then about four months into the relationship, I go by her mom's house to see her and she has a black eye."
"Oh, my God," Carol gasped and looked at Lisa.

"That's not it. Then shit really gets hectic, she completely stops hanging out with me and Pat. From what her mother was telling me, she stopped hanging out with family too."

"You don't have to talk like I'm not even here," Lisa said, while pouring herself another glass of wine.

"Anyway, he would keep track of everything she did and everywhere she went. I have to admit, she didn't let him ruin her chance of pursuing her degree. I'm so glad she didn't. But –"

"Can I tell my own story, please?" Lisa said, cutting Nic off.

"Sure, as long as it's the truth," Nic said.

Lisa stuck her tongue out at Nic, and then said, "When I met James, I hadn't been in a relationship in about four years. The last guy I dated I was really heartbroken over, and I was still sort of waiting for him to come back. Anyway, as she said, at the beginning everything was fine. We would go out to movies, clubs, and restaurants, anything else you could think of. I was so attracted to him, so I overlooked a lot of things. Come on, even though he is evil, you saw him Carol."

Carol nodded.

"At the time, I was overweight, so someone as good looking as him showing me some interest made me feel like I was the most beautiful woman in the world. And he was older than me, so he knew how to get my young ass."

"How much older is he then you?" Carol said.

"About ten years," Lisa said. "I was nineteen, so I didn't have a lot of life experience. All I knew was going to school and what I learned from this old hooker," Lisa laughed, as she pointed at Nic.

"Whatever," Nic said, throwing a pillow at Lisa.

"So after four months, things started to change."

"Four months?" Carol asked.

"Yeah, I mean, he already knew he had me. He knew all my weaknesses and even used them to get me on his side. Then he started getting meaner and wanting to spend every waking moment together. It began to be too much, it seemed like every time he would walk in he would suck all the air out of the room. It started to feel like there wasn't any room for me to breathe anymore. And I did stop hanging out with my friends and family. I just told them that I had a lot of homework. My mother tried to talk some sense into me, but of course I wouldn't listen. By then the pushing and slapping had started and I was afraid to tell my mother. Considering she never liked him, I couldn't tell her that he was hitting on me."

"Yeah, by the end Mrs. Janice was talking about killing that fool," Nic said.

"As always, after every fight, he would be so sorry and I would believe him."

"I know this is probably a stupid question, but why would you forgive him? I mean, you don't seem to be that type of person," Carol said.

"I'm not now, but I was. It took some time for me to get here and I'm truly blessed to be."

"I've heard some people say that after they slept together, that's when the person changed. Is that what happened to you?"

"No. To be honest, it had been a minute for me, if you know what I mean. So it didn't take long for us to sleep together; to be more accurate, two weeks. He was gorgeous, I couldn't help it. He got to me through conversation. We could talk about anything. That's what attracted me. But it's not like he didn't know what he was doing. He knew how to get to me. He had me believing that he was the man for me. Scratch that, I had myself believing that he was the man for me. I was addicted to him. Hell, part of me still is! Shut up, Nic."

"I didn't say anything," Nic said.

"So what happened to make you finally leave him?" Carol asked.

"He almost killed her," Nic said.

"What?" Carol shrieked, looking at Lisa.

Lisa took a deep breath and said, "We were having problems, as usual, and I got tired of it. I wasn't allowed to go anywhere unless he was with me. So I told him it was over and that I couldn't go through this over and over again. At first he said he loved me and that he would straighten up. I told him I didn't believe him and that we couldn't keep going on like this. When he realized I wasn't going to change my mind, he decided to beat me until I did. He started to punch, slap, kick and everything else he wanted to do me. Apparently, he had knocked me out, because when I woke up it was two weeks later. I was in the hospital with six broken ribs, a concussion, two black eyes and I couldn't remember what happened."

"What happened to him? Did he go to jail?" Carol asked.

"It's kind of fuzzy, but Ms. Detective here can fill you in. I have to go to the bathroom," Lisa said, getting up off the floor.

When Lisa was out of hearing range, Nic finished the story. "During her two weeks in a coma all the pieces came together. The beating happened at his house and afterward he left her there. When she didn't come home the night before, her mother called me and asked if I had seen her? When I told her no, she really got worried. No one knew where he stayed. I'd just go on the police department and decided to put his name in the system. We got his address and I met her mother over at his house. When we got there the door was unlocked, and when we opened the door she was laying on the floor. I tell you, Carol, when we found her she looked dead and was close to it. The ambulance got there in time to keep her breathing, but, Carol, I have to tell you we didn't think she was going to make it. There was so much blood. I put out his description, but no one could find him."

"How did you find him then?"

"A couple of days had passed before he showed up at the hos-pital. He thought everyone had left and snuck into her room, but to his surprise I was waiting on his ass."

"You think he came to finish what he started?"

"I really do."

"Then you saved her life."

"That's my girl. If I couldn't get to her before it happened, I made damn sure it wouldn't happen again. Anyway, he pled guilty to a lesser charge and only got three years, while she's scarred for life.

Carol and Nic sat quietly until Lisa walked back into the room.

"What time is it?" Carol asked.

"Ten o'clock, ladies," Lisa said.

"It's just ten and I'm already drunk." Carol laughed.

"Me, too," Lisa and Nic said in unison, and then they all started laughing.

"Well neither of you are leaving under these conditions, so get comfortable," Lisa said.

"Girl, I already have. I packed a bag before I left home," Carol said.

"And I don't have to be at work until two tomorrow afternoon," said Nic, as she refilled her glass.

Then an idea came to Lisa. "Carol, has any good gossip been going around the office lately?"

"You mean about you and Mr. Cavell?"
"Say what?" Nic said.
"Oh yes, honey. They are the talk of the office."
"What is everyone saying?" asked Lisa.
"Right now, just petty stuff… Nothing of any credit."
"Petty stuff like what?"
"Actually they're saying you and Mr. Cavell have been looking very chummy these days and that no matter how much the women in the office try, they don't get anywhere with him. Especially, that Miss Wanna-be Melody. She has been trying to get his attention since she started working at the firm last year."
"Have they ever gone out?" Lisa asked, hoping that the tone of jealousy wasn't evident. But, both Carol and Nic noticed.
Then Carol said, "Why, you don't want him. Shit, let somebody else have his fine ass."
"I know you've had too much to drink now, because I am not interested in Marc."
"Yeah right! All I know is that you better make up your mind, because the vultures are circling honey," Carol said.
"Lisa, you know the man likes you. Hell, that time we ran into him while shopping I could tell. He barely acknowledged me and you know that shit just does not happen," Nic said, as she flipped her hair over her shoulder.
"Anyway, Miss Thang, I told you that I was concentrating on my career."
"We've heard it all before," said Nic.
That conversation went on well into the night. Looking at the clock, Lisa realized it was two o'clock in the morning. By two-thirty the living room and kitchen were clean and everyone had their sleeping assignments.
Lisa stood in the hallway of the facing rooms and asked, "Does everybody have what they need?"
"Yes, ma'am," Nic said in a little girl voice and all of them started laughing.
"Alright, ladies. Good night."
"Good night," Nic and Carol said.
The minute Lisa finished her prayers, she fell asleep. That night Lisa dreamed of making love to James. In her dream, they were in a room

filled with candles on a large bed with silk white sheets. As Lisa straddled his lap, he kissed her deeply and passionately, as she came and called his name. When they rolled over, Lisa looked into James eyes as he continued to kiss her and bring her to an ecstasy that she never experienced. As James went deeper, he said, "I love you Lisa." Lisa jumped up to the sound of her alarm going off. She was more tired now than when she went to sleep. She hit the button on the alarm clock and got up to start her day.

Final Thoughts

The writers of Voices Behind the Tears along with Saving Lives Through Lit, would like to thank you for taking the time and supporting our cause with the purchase of this book. We ask that you please visit and join both our web site and FB page as well as spread the word. Domestic Violence is more than a one a year cause, it's an everyday occurrence for many, many people, who deserve that we do our due diligence as often as possible to raise awareness.

Together as a nation, a country, a society, a world, we can take what is the norm, the secret, the accepted and turn it around. The Abusers NOT the Victims should be the ones feeling embarrassed. Please reach out to someone you know who may be hurting, or going through. Give them a hug; tell them you are there whenever they are ready to get out. Let them know you understand it's not easy. Give comfort to a child enduring the hardship of seeing their parent abused, or one who has themselves been abused. It is NEVER okay to beat a child black and blue, to grab anyone by their hair, to punch them and call them obscene names. Yet, we turn a blind eye, when our family members to this to their children or to their loved ones.

Until we wake up and realize no matter who the abuser is, the abuse will only continue to escalate. Bullying, Belittling, Physical, Emotional, Sexual, Spousal abuse, are ALL WRONG!

Wake up and let's put an end to this…Together!

Saving Lives Through Lit

LINKS:
Savinglivesthroughlit.org
Twitter.com/litsavinglives
Facebook.com/savinglivesthroughlit
Myspace.com/savinglivesthroughlit
Linkedin.com/in/savinglivesthroughlit
Youtube.com/litsavinglives

Special Thanks

To the talented writers, poets, authors who shared their talent with us, we thank you for the courage to reach deep and pull out the wonderful expressions that you shared with the world!

Elizabeth Funderbirk-Rowe
Robert Sells
Tamari Toledo
Michele Tooles
Carlet Horne
Lavinia Thompson
Chamani J Carter
Tamyara Brown
Terrell Mercer
Tony Wade
Envy Red
Joyce Oscar
C. Highsmith-Hooks
 Charron Monaye
Taquila Thompson
 Latisha Patterson
Mashawn Mickles
Meka "Phoenix" Carter
N.S. Ngezene
Poetic Swag
Mahogani P.
Antoinette Lakey
Danielle "Dani" Taylor
Ernestine Moore
Laura Johnson

Kiexiza Rodriquez
Karen "Kaye" Stackfield
GPA
 Luna Charles
 W. Kay Shabazz
 Kelli Garden

Sponsors

To those that donated their time, energy, and services to making this project a success, we could not have pulled this off as well as we did without your help! For your interviews, features, designs and so much more, we humbly thank you!

Donna Osborn Clark
Glenda Wallace
Funderbirk-Rowe Family
Destiny Carter
The Stutts/Green Family
Michelle Green
Lisa-Tyrrell Amos-Perry
The Dub Spot
The Taylor Family
Adrienna Turner
The 1 Essence
Lateef Ade' Reid

Please check out and support the businesses that supported and helped this anthology be created...

CreationByDonna.com
Pinkkisspublishing.com
Literaryliz.com
Emeraldstarpress.net
Diamondstarentertainment.webs.com
Safehavenpubco.com
Wordondastreet.jimdo.com
Sofyhmagazineonline.com
Dream4morewebs.com
The1essence.com
Crmnlelements.blogspot.com

www.ingramcontent.com/pod-product-compliance
Lightning Source LLC
LaVergne TN
LVHW051827080426
835512LV00018B/2753